THE NARCISSIST NEXT DOOR: AN INTIMATE LOOK AT NARCISSISTIC CULTURE

Heather Sheafer

Page Turner Press

TABLE OF CONTENTS

Part I

NARCISSISM DEFINED

Chapter 1

WHAT IS NARCISSISM?

"For the most part people are not curious except about themselves."

– John Steinbeck, *The Winter of Our Discontent*

"Part of me suspects that I'm a loser,
and the other part of me thinks I'm God Almighty."

– John Lennon

On May 23, 1934, Clyde Barrow and Bonnie Parker were shot to death by Louisiana Police after a three day manhunt. The couple was wanted by the FBI for a long list of crimes across five states, including robbery, kidnapping and at least thirteen murders. Although the couple's crimes were heinous, they are remembered nearly 80 years later for their odd behavior during their years evading justice. Most notably, Clyde was willing to do anything for his own self-interest. He killed anyone who got in his way. In order to obtain an early prison release for medical care, he cut off two of his own toes. While on the run, Clyde stole cars frequently to remain undetected by police. A very particular car thief, he was willing to kill for a car but only stole Fords. In the month before his death, Clyde wrote a letter to Henry Ford, praising the car's speedy V8 engine.

It is not known if Bonnie actively killed anyone, but she did enjoy writing poetry and bragging about her exploits. Although Bonnie's upbringing had been entirely ordinary, her poetry expressed a belief that she and her lover would be remembered after death. And perhaps, the part of Bonnie and Clyde's story most strongly imbedded in popular culture: the photos. A raid of the couple's apartment shortly before their death turned up a roll of film. In spite of being actively involved in a deadly crime spree, the pair made time to pose playfully with their guns and cars.[1]

More recently, Christopher Dorner captured the world's attention in a similar, albeit shorter and more carefully organized killing spree. In February of 2013, Dorner killed four people, including two police officers, and injured three other officers. Dorner was an ex-police officer who felt he had been unfairly dismissed from his position. Shortly before the killings began, Dorner posted a 20-page manifesto to his Facebook page. Addressed broadly to America, the letter described his actions as a "necessary evil." It is unclear whether Dorner's firing from the Los Angeles Police Department was, in fact, unfair and the department has struggled with accusations of corruption for decades; but Dorner's manifesto made it clear that he viewed himself being up against the world, and that he over-evaluated himself while devaluing others. The manhunt for Dorner, which was the largest in Los Angeles Police Department history, ended when he took his own life in a mountain cabin during a police stand-off.[2]

History tends to remember sensational people, such as Bonnie Parker, Clyde Barrow, Christopher Dorner and dozens of other infamous criminals as textbook narcissists. Narcissistic Personality Disorder (NPD) is described by the Diagnostic and Statistical Manual of Mental Disorders (DSM-5) as "a pattern of grandiosity, need for admiration, and lack of empathy." It goes on to describe narcissists as having a "tendency to be tough-minded, glib, superficial, exploitative, and unempathic."[3] Certainly, several infamous people fit this description. But, don't other people meet the criteria? People whom others might consider "normal?"

To some degree, all people have narcissistic traits, and some degree of narcissism is normal and necessary for healthy self-esteem. At what point does it become a disorder? Can teachers, doctors, actors and parents be narcissists? Do narcissists have to be sociopaths? In fact, the DSM-5 is clear that although it can occur, NPD is not necessarily characterized by aggression or deceit. The truth is that plenty of "normal" people living "normal" lives are living with NPD.[3]

Characteristics of a Narcissist

Narcissism comes in two flavors: cerebral or somatic. The cerebral narcissist derives a sense of superiority from intelligence and academic performance, whereas the somatic narcissist's self-image comes from sexual prowess, physical appearance, and material possessions.[8] Although narcissism is experienced differently by each individual, most narcissists share a common set of traits.

Attention-Seeking. Narcissists love to be the center of attention. Additionally, they believe they *deserve* to be the center of attention. Oftentimes, they become hurt or angry when they do not receive the attention or admiration they feel they deserve.

Superficial Charm. As social chameleons, narcissists frequently seem to be charming. Often, a narcissist will realize that he or she will gain more attention or social approval by behaving in a humble way, and feign humility. In this way and others, narcissists are social chameleons. They can adjust their personalities to meet current social needs, and even though they don't care to understand the feelings of others, they can usually guess what they need to do to please someone at a superficial level. A common tactic for showing off while simultaneously playing humble is to feign ignorance about a given subject. For example, a narcissist may say he knows nothing about a specific current event when in fact, he is very familiar. When the details are explained, the narcissist can then appear to catch on quickly. The same is true for sports and other activities. A narcissist may say, "I've never played tennis" so that he can appear to be an extremely talented novice.

Grandiose Sense of Self. When they are successful, narcissists tend to devalue the contributions of others. Narcissists typically believe they are special or unique and expect to be treated as such. When a narcissist successfully breaks a rule without consequence, he often believes that it is his special status, not luck or mercy that allowed him to get away with bad behavior. When things go badly, it is attributed to the failures or shortcoming of others. They tend to compare themselves with famous or accomplished people and often believe that only other "special" people can understand them. They also insist on only associating with the "best." For example, a narcissist may only want to be treated by the "best" doctor or expect to go to the "best" college. In personal conversation, the narcissist will always "one-up" the person he is talking to. His experience is always better or worse, and he perceives this as an extension of his personal value. For example, many years ago, I showed my new car to a friend who displayed narcissistic traits. The exchange must have made him feel insecure about his car because he started bragging about minute details: "How many cup holders does your car have? Mine has 12." Then he dragged me to his car to prove that his air conditioner was colder than mine.

Because narcissists tend to devalue others, it is a common misconception that a narcissist will think he is better or harder working than his friends. Often, this is not the case, at least externally. A person with NPD desires successful friends. They often believe that a relationship is more intimate than it is. For example, a narcissist may meet the president of his company once during a work event and later tell others they are close friends.

In the same way, narcissists are often drawn to religion. After all, who is better to know than God? Adherence to religious ideals helps the narcissist appear to be good. Religion offers another handy tool to the narcissist. A person with NPD is typically aware of his bad behavior. A systematic method of receiving forgiveness after a transgression is greatly useful in cleaning the narcissist's slate. A strong desire to be part of a group can lead a narcissist into religion, and sometimes into a cult.

Fragile Sense of Self-Esteem. Although narcissists appear to have a very strong sense of self-esteem, their self-image is extremely fragile and can be damaged by any number of circumstances going wrong. True self-esteem is derived from an individual's accomplishments and a sense of being true to self, especially when facing adversity. Narcissism comes from a sense of entitlement, not self-esteem. When a narcissist's feelings are hurt, he is apt to counter-attack. Criticism can trouble a narcissist for years, creating feelings of emptiness or humiliation.

Sense of Entitlement. Narcissists tend to believe that rules don't apply to them. For example, a narcissist may have a difficult time waiting in a long line or may become angry when a restaurant loses his or her dinner reservation. Narcissists are also inclined to criticize or label others, especially when they don't get their way. Narcissists are often perfectionists and demand that people around them do things their way. These behaviors often lead to narcissists being viewed as snobby or arrogant. Narcissists can become deeply offended when social graces are not reciprocated. Many narcissists engage in "mind reading," which essentially is deciding they understand another person's motive. Assume a friend does not call you back immediately after you leave a message. You can probably go a few days without feeling as though you have been rejected. *It's the weekend,* you may tell yourself. *He's had a tough week and is probably enjoying time with his family.* A narcissist, on the other hand, will take this as a personal rejection. Of course, there are plenty of circumstances under which you may feel rejected, but this is a common occurrence for a person with NPD.

Impaired Empathy. Narcissists have an extremely difficult time understanding the needs of others. They often assume that others are as interested in their personal needs as they are. In conversation, a narcissist is likely to talk about him or herself at length and become impatient when others talk about themselves. Because narcissists lack empathy, they might talk about themselves to the point of hurting others without being aware. For example, a narcissist may brag about her healthy marriage to a friend going through divorce. When a friend or relative points out hurtful behavior in a person with NPD , the narcissist may respond by characterizing the person as overly-sensitive or to not intelligent enough to understand.

Exploitativeness. The combination of being unable to feel empathy and a desire to further one's self-interest often puts narcissists in a position of unknowingly taking advantage of or exploiting others. Because narcissists avoid intimacy, they have an easy time detaching from friends and family who offend them or are no longer useful to them. Narcissists often deal with feelings of jealousy and suspect that others are jealous of them. Jealousy occurs when another person has the material possessions, success or recognition that an individual with NPD believes he or she deserves. Because they feel superior to others, it seems only natural that others would be jealous or try to take advantage. Narcissists typically choose friendships or romantic partners based on what can be obtained socially or financially from the relationship.

Problems with Intimacy. Narcissists are infamous for marrying multiple times. A healthy person who has been divorced two or three times can think of reasons why marriage may not be a good choice in the future. "I'm just not cut out for marriage" is a common sentiment after a second divorce. The narcissist, however, sees himself as perfectly cut out for marriage. It is the spouse, of course, who created the trouble. An extreme but recent example is the story of Drew Peterson. When Peterson's fourth wife, Stacey disappeared in 2007, investigators discovered that the death of his third wife, Kathleen Savio, was also extremely suspicious. Kathleen was found dead in a dry bathtub shortly after the couple's divorce. Peterson was found guilty of Kathleen's murder and sentenced to 38 years in prison. Stacey Peterson's body was never found. Peterson made several mistakes consistent with narcissism. First, he failed to see how his own behaviors and decisions led to the collapse of each marriage. This detachment allowed him to marry four times. His fifth fiancée left him during the murder investigation. Second, he treated each wife as a disposable object, figuratively at first, and eventually literally. Next, he believed he was above the law. After literally getting away with murder, Peterson felt he was untouchable. Peterson's final narcissistic mistake was talking and joking freely with the press, ignoring the advice of his attorneys. Criminals who go out of their way to discuss a pending legal matter are almost always displaying narcissistic tendencies, if not NPD. Of course, as discussed earlier, NPD does not make a person violent. In most narcissists, this pattern of being open to or seeking attention in situations from which most sensible people would retreat is prevalent.

Narcissism in Children and Adolescents

Self-esteem in children can be relatively tricky. Infants and toddlers feel naturally as though they are the center of the universe, an evolutionary necessity for survival. In older children, self-esteem is typically based on accomplishments and internal circumstances rather than external circumstances. Folk wisdom tells us that parents desire a child with high self-esteem and that high self-esteem is symptomatic of a happy childhood. It is also normal for small children to have an inflated sense of their own abilities and potential. Most children, for example, will tell you they plan to be an astronaut, princess, or President of the United States rather than an accountant or a plumber. Young children also have an inflated sense of their parents' abilities. For example, a toddler may brag, "my dad is the strongest person in the world." These are all symptoms of healthy self-esteem in children. An important distinction between the fantasies of healthy children and the fantasy of children with NPD is that healthy children accept that other children can share their aspirations and bragging rights. A child with NPD will believe that he or she can be a baseball player or a famous actress because of an *innate superiority*.

Childhood Narcissism and Self-Esteem

Narcissism is symptomatic of low self-esteem in children. Signs of childhood narcissism are similar to signs of adult narcissism, including lack of empathy, a sense of superiority, and behaviors consistent with entitlement. All children have a need for attention and admiration, but narcissistic children can never seem to have their needs met. All children struggle with failure or not getting their way, but healthy children recover emotionally. Narcissistic children often hide their shortcomings by lying, and when that isn't possible-- they respond by retreating, making excuses or becoming enraged. Narcissistic lies are different than normal childhood fantasies, as they are designed to make the child feel better than his or her peers. These feelings and behaviors are a defensive response to feelings of powerlessness and worthlessness.[4] For example, Lance was a 9-year-old boy who could not lose at games without experiencing an assault on his self-worth. When a neighbor girl won during a game of one-on-one basketball, he told her that he was used to playing with a much higher basketball hoop and the lower hoop was "too easy." He then left the game and refused to play again. Lance's behavior was consistent, no matter the game. If he couldn't win, he was instantly defensive and would leave, under the pretense of being too advanced for the activity. He also felt a need to "one-up" his peers. When a friend was cast in a school play, Lance devalued the boy's accomplishments by telling him that he had twice as many lines when he was in a play. Healthy children are able to be happy for their peers and do not see the success of others as a threat, particularly when not competing.

Similarly, children with NPD have little patience for any task at which they are not instantly successful. This often presents in later childhood, when schoolwork becomes more challenging and new academic tasks, such as learning an instrument or a new language is expected. Lance began having problems in school and was required to repeat 5th grade after doing well in earlier grades. He was quick to blame external circumstances; an unsupportive teacher and principal who were out to get him, classmates who distracted him, his move to new school years before.

When a child with NPD is up against a wall and cannot deflect blame with his typical toolkit of excuses and diversions, he lays on self-deprecating dramatics. These children cry loudly so that the entire family can hear. They often say awful things about themselves, declaring themselves stupid, bad and worthless. This is a two-fold strategy. First, the narcissistic child has extremely fragile self-esteem. Being caught and forced to deal with consequences may never really get a child to face his mistakes, but the child must deal with his inability to control the situation in which he was caught. Second, self-deprecating dramatics are a last-ditch effort to manipulate parents or other authority figures. Riley, an 11-year-old-girl, was caught ditching school more than once. Her mother and school authorities developed an appropriate discipline plan. Once Riley threw herself on her bed and began screaming that she was stupid and worthless, her mother began to re-think the consequences. *Riley sure seemed sorry. She made a mistake, but she feels awful and truly understands how wrong she was. She won't do it again.* Within hours, Riley was out of her room, with full reign of the house, cuddling with her mother and discussing dinner plans. Riley, of course, got to choose dinner since she had gone through such an awful day.

As in younger children, traits of narcissism are often displayed in and developmentally appropriate in teenagers of both sexes. Adolescence is a time when most young people develop a sense of self-worth as they navigate circumstances that can result in embarrassment and shame. Typically, teenagers adjust their behavior to the reactions of their social groups, and narcissistic behaviors are corrected by adulthood.[5]

Who has NPD and Why?

Only about 1% of the general population is diagnosed with NPD, although prevalence is much higher among people already treated for psychological disorders. Up to 75% of narcissists are men. Narcissists are more likely than the general population to abuse alcohol, and half of all narcissists will struggle with alcoholism or other substance abuse during their lifespan. Although research examining the connection between alcoholism and narcissism dates back to 1945, it is hard to determine whether narcissism causes alcoholism, or if alcoholism creates a narcissist.[6]

Childhood narcissism is often mistaken for attention deficit hyperactivity disorder (ADHD). Interestingly, adult ADHD is highly correlated with alcoholism, the most common disorder co-diagnosed with NPD. In general, almost all personality disorders are diagnosed in conjunction with another disorder. For the average every day narcissist, substance abuse, ADHD, depression and anxiety are most common.[7] The sensational narcissists, the ones we learn about only after a violent crime has been committed, are usually suffering from a combination of NPD and antisocial personality disorder (ASPD). Although NPD can impair feelings of empathy, antisocial personality is more closely related to violent and criminal behavior. Similarly, narcissistic children and teenagers who have violent tendencies are typically co-diagnosed with conduct disorder. Behaviors common to conduct disorder include bullying, threatening, fighting and cruelty to people and animals. Children and teens who run away, vandalize, use weapons, steal directly from another person, sexually assault others and kill are almost always presenting conduct disorder. All of these symptoms and disorders can present with or without narcissistic tendencies.

Maternal Attachment and Narcissism

Although several conflicting theories have attempted to explain the causes of narcissism, almost professionals believe that the roots usually extend from the narcissist's mother being unable to meet emotional needs during infancy and early childhood.[8] This can be confusing, because oftentimes, the narcissist's mother may seem doting, even indulgent. An emotionally absent mother can be more subtle and complex than a mother who abandons her child or who is absent. In many cases, a loving mother is preoccupied by uncontrollable life circumstances and therefore unable to meet her child's emotional needs. Non-abusive circumstances can include the mother being in a difficult or toxic relationship, a single or impoverished mother who must spend extended time away in order to support her family, or a mother who has many other children in her care.

When this is discussed in therapy, patients who have good relationships with their mothers are often quick to blame their father. *My dad left when I was 2, my mother was always there for me.* Or, *My father was a raging alcoholic, my mother was the one who cared for me.* In such toxic upbringings, a well-meaning mother may have too much on her plate and become emotionally unavailable, even when physically present. A loving mother who is doing her best to raise a child under difficult circumstances may rightfully be concerned for her child's self-esteem. These efforts can be manifested as excessive unconditional praise, linking a child's efforts or achievements to the child's self-worth, and letting the child believe he or she is special, or more deserving than other children.[9]

Common Origins of Narcissism

Although the origins of narcissism within the personality are difficult to determine, studies of childhood narcissism have identified specific circumstances common in children with NPD. Children at high-risk for narcissistic tendencies include children who are over-indulged, or spoiled by their parents, children of divorced parents, adopted children, and children whose parents are exceptionally talented or successful.

First, parents of spoiled or over-indulged children are consistently reinforcing the child's belief of being special or above the rules. This was the case with Lance. Lance's mother "stood up" for him whenever he ran into problems at school. She complained that he was being bullied when he didn't have friends, and ran to the principal when the teacher didn't treat him the way she believed he deserved to be treated. She attributed his poor grades to not being challenged and switched him to a different school when he was to repeat the 5th grade. When he was caught with marijuana at school, his mother told the school it belonged to a family member and he had no idea what it was. When Riley was caught cheating on a test, her mother felt that canceling her birthday party the following weekend was "too harsh." When Riley was doing poorly in her music class, her mother asked that she be switched to another instrument. Both Lance and Riley had friendship problems, and both of their mothers labeled the exclusion as bullying. Instead of working on improving each child's social skills, both mothers blamed the other children, even contacting the school and other parents and demanding inclusion for their children.

Children of divorced parents face similar circumstances. When parents engage in a custody battle, they are apt to spoil the child in hopes of winning favor and treat the child as though he or she is a prize to be won. In cases where the parents are amicable or one parent is absent, the child may devalue the parent who does not meet his or her needs. Adopted children need not be spoiled to experience an inflated sense of worth. It has become fashionable to help adoptive children overcome feelings of rejection from their biological parents by telling them that being adopted makes them special because they were chosen. This can create a sense of superiority over children being raised by their biological parents, particularly if the child is being raised with siblings who are not adopted. Finally, children whose parents are particularly successful or talented may feel as though they, too, are naturally destined to become successful or talented. Painful feelings of inadequacy can be manifested as narcissistic tendencies. Have you ever been shocked to learn that a child of a famous person has been arrested or an heiress has made a sex tape? You probably considered the productive choices you could have made if only you had that level of privilege. In reality, a high level of privilege combined with minimal talent can create narcissistic tendencies.[9]

Along these lines is the theory that narcissism stems from inadequate frustrating experiences during childhood. A parent who tries to protect a child from frustration is robbing him or her of opportunities to accept and adapt to limitations and create healthy boundaries.[10]

Conversely, narcissism can also come from an upbringing fraught with coldness, high or unfair expectations and lack of support. In these cases, the child develops an inflated, narcissistic self-view to protect him or herself against feelings of rejection. These children also seek attention from adults and peers who can provide them with warmth and validation. This can eventually lead to a dependence of external, rather than internal, sources to affirm self-views.[9] A classic, Freud-era conceptualization of narcissism sees it as a result of physical abuse, when threat to the child's body comes before the child is able to see himself as safe and whole.

Of course, not every child raised under these circumstances exhibits narcissistic tendencies or develops them in adulthood. Many experts believe that narcissism can be inherited and is one of the most heritable personality disorders. This approach asserts that narcissism is rooted in biologically-based temperamental traits. Environmental conditions, as discussed previously, can activate these biologically-driven traits. For example, a person with a naturally outgoing, energetic and sensation-seeking temperament is likely at greater risk for narcissistic traits than a naturally shy personality. The specific cause of any psychiatric disorder is unknown and, in most cases, a unique combination of genetics and environmental conditions create a disorder. The social psychology view called *equifinality* indicates that multiple developmental pathways can lead to a specific trait or disorder.[9]

Chapter 2

A BRIEF HISTORY OF NARCISSISM

"The desire to annoy no one, to harm no one, can equally well be the sign of a just as of an anxious disposition."

– Friedrich Nietzsche

"If you want to be proud of yourself, than do things in which you can take pride."

– Karen Horney, *Neurosis and Human Growth: The Struggle Towards Self-Realization*

As with many psychological disorders, narcissism was named after a Greek myth. Narcissus, the son of a blue nymph named Leiriope and a predatory river god named Cephisus, was beautiful from birth. According to legend, his beauty was such that both men and women fell in love with him before he was old enough to take his first steps.

The only member of the community who could not see Narcissus' beauty was Teiresias, a bisexual man who was condemned to eternal blindness after losing a bet to Zeus. Without use of his eyes, Teiresias was able to see into the future and use his sexual experience with both men and women to advise others. Leiriope, concerned for her son's future asked Teiresias if Narcissus would enjoy a long life. Teiresias advised that he would, as long as he never comes to know himself. Teiresias' prediction proved true when Narcissus fell in love with his own reflection and died next to the spring because he was unable to leave the sight of his own beauty.[11]

Before Narcissus died alone, his self-love destroyed at least two romantic relationships. Echo loved him dearly, but was painfully rejected. After crossing Zeus' wife, Hera, Echo was afflicted with a curse that limited her speech to only repeating what was last said to her. Narcissus physically threw the nymph from his body and told her he would rather die than be with her. Echo went into a deep depression after being cast off so cruelly. Unable to eat or sleep, her body eventually died, leaving only her voice behind. Ameinias, another potential lover, killed himself with a sword after being unable to attain Narcissus' love. His final words set a curse, willing that Narcissus become obsessed with a love he himself could not attain. It was shortly after this curse that Narcissus came upon a beautiful spring that had never been visited by animals or disturbed even by the droppings of trees. It did not take long for him to become mesmerized by the beautiful youth who looked up at him from the clear, silvery spring. His desire turned to frustration when he was unable to kiss the beautiful face. He was unable to keep himself from falling in when he reached out to hold the young man's body. Narcissus knew that the boy below the water wanted him, too. Every time he moved in for a kiss, so did the reflection. Every time he stretched his arms towards his love, the boy reciprocated.[11]

Eventually, Narcissus realized that his star-crossed lover was in fact himself! Instead of making a decision to move on, or perhaps mend past relationships (at this point, Echo was still close at hand, helping him whenever possible), Narcissus found himself in a more complex conundrum than before. He didn't know if he should continue to be the pursuer, or allow his own reflection to woo him. He was grief stricken by the notion that he could never have what he wanted most, and prayed to be separated from his body. His only comfort during this time was that his new lover would remain true to him and never leave.[11]

After years of staying by his reflection's side, Narcissus' beauty began to diminish. His fair skin burned, his youth faded, and years of lying upon a river bank left him thin and weakened. With Echo still by his side, Narcissus plunged a dagger into his heart, and died alongside his reflection .[11]

Throughout history, particularly as psychology began to develop as a science, views of narcissism have changed. Still it is interesting that a caricature of reality, which is Narcissus' story, can so closely relate to the experiences of narcissistic men and women today. Narcissus had opportunities for loving relationships, but his self-love made it impossible for him to engage. Echo, who was essentially helpless in the relationship, did everything she could to love and support Narcissus, even through years of him being unable to reciprocate. Once Narcissus understood that the problem plaguing his life was himself *him*, he was still unable to make the changes necessary to reciprocate love. Ultimately, Narcissus' demise came when his shallow sense of self-worth was no longer valuable. His looks and youth were gone and he had nothing more to live for.

Early Psychoanalytical Theory and Narcissism

By the turn of the 20th century, theorists Paul Nacke and Havelock Ellis had both used the term "narcissism" to describe any person who treated his own body as a sexual object. During this era, masturbation was viewed as a perversion, and any patient who admitted to self-stimulation was diagnosable. Victorian research concluded that narcissistic traits were found primarily in homosexual men. Like other theorists of his time, Sigmund Freud made little distinction between homosexuality and narcissism. Both were considered perverse and both conditions were characterized by obsessive self-involvement, arrested development, inability to love, disdain for the opposite sex, and shallow values, beliefs and ideas.[12] The argument for narcissism being inherently homosexual during early psychoanalysis came from the belief that a sexual relationship with a person of the same sex was the closest one could get to having sex with himself. This is incredibly narrow, of course, considering that people of any sexual orientation can distinguish the difference between themselves and others outside gender and genitalia. During these early theories, other individual differences, such as race, and relational factors, such as conversations and common interests, were not considered.

Early Theories Regarding Childhood Development of Narcissism

Freud's daughter, Anna Freud, was a psychoanalytical theorist who worked for years with childhood survivors of concentration camps. In an extension of her father's theory that all male sexuality stems from early maternal relationships, she theorized that a healthy mother "seduces" her infant from his self-love. When a mother is unavailable, either emotionally or physically, the child cannot make the change from self-love narcissism to healthy object-love narcissism. The child is stuck in an infantile phase characterized by self-pleasure.[11] Sigmund Freud asserted that narcissism is a normal part of early childhood development, and only problematic when continued into adulthood. Even today, experts who work with children notice that self-centeredness is a normal part of the toddler years, when children are cognitively unable to understand the needs of others.

Otto Kernberg asserted that narcissism was the result of an emotionally-devaluing childhood environment fraught with rejection. The parents of a narcissist were painted as inconsistent, cold and dismissive, but able to "switch on" warmth and attentiveness to suit their own needs. This theory stated that narcissism offers the child a reprieve from a reality fraught with shame and emptiness.

Heinz Kohut, on the other hand, viewed narcissism as a disruption to the development of healthy self-esteem. Similar to Freud, Kohut viewed grandiosity as a normal childhood experience and narcissism as an inability to regulate and successfully apply it in adulthood.[13]

Case Studies in Narcissism

The first case study that described the narcissistic personality the way we see it today was published by Ralph Walder in 1925. Walder described his patient as feeling superior to others, sexually selfish, and unwilling to connect emotional intimacy to his sexuality. His patient was also obsessed with admiration and had a difficult time experiencing feelings of empathy. Shortly after, Freud and psychoanalyst Wilhelm Reich expanded narcissism to include coldness, aggression, and ill humor. Karen Horney was the first theorist to carefully distinguish healthy levels of narcissism from pathological narcissism. Specifically, she explained that the narcissistic personality has no real foundation for his self-love, value and admiration. Unlike Freud, who believed that a narcissist's self-love was genuine, Horney viewed the narcissist's self-love as defensive and asserted that the narcissist is incapable of genuine love for himself or others.[13] By the 1970s, narcissism was recognized as a disorder across theoretical orientation, and its underpinnings had been examined.

Conceptualization of Narcissistic Personality Disorder

Largely regarded as the bible of mental illness, *The Diagnostic and Statistical Manual* (DSM) was the first comprehensive publication to list and classify mental disorders. The DSM-1, published by the American Psychiatric Association (APA) in 1952, listed and described 106 disorders, with no concrete diagnostic information or regard to interrelations among disorders.[14] Additionally, the descriptions of disorders and their causes in the DSM-I were heavily influenced by psychoanalytic theory. These features made diagnoses across the field difficult and inconsistent.[15]

In 1968, DSM-II listed and described 182 psychological disorders. Few improvements were made over the previous version, but the diagnoses were compatible with the International Classification of Diseases (ICD), the system used by the World Health Organization (WHO) to classify medical illnesses. Still, the theories and diagnoses presented in DSM-II did not closely resemble medical diagnoses. During the 1970s, the APA set out to develop a new DSM that carefully presented symptoms, prognosis, clinical course, and treatment responses to disorders that spanned several meticulously designed categories. When the DSM-III was published in 1980, the authors knew they were a long way from identifying biological markers associated with psychological illnesses. Nevertheless, they were successful in presenting algorithmic, observable indicators of disease and process,[15] while intentionally omitting ties to any specific theory.[14] The DSM-III was controversial, especially among psychoanalysts whose theoretical orientation was no longer central to DSM. Despite opposition from within the field, DSM-III was triumphant in gaining respect for psychiatry as a science within the medical field. It was in this version of the DSM that narcissistic personality disorder (NPD) was officially introduced. Because the new manual was a departure from psychoanalytical theory, its description represented a research-based approach to NPD that differed from the works of both Kernberg and Kohut. A revision of the third edition, DSM-III-R was published in 1987, describing 292 diagnoses.[15] Increase in diagnoses over previous revisions of the manual was attributed to more carefully defined subtypes, and increase in descriptive research in addition to the creation of new disorders.[14] The manual gained popularity, and before long was the undisputed authority on mental illness, even if its flaws--primarily low reliability, were recognized.[15]

Under the DSM-III, A diagnosis of NPD required that the patient experience the following four traits as part of current and long-term functioning:

1) Grandiose sense of self-importance or uniqueness, e.g., exaggeration of achievements and talents, focus on the

special nature of one's problem.

2) Preoccupation with fantasies of unlimited success, power, brilliance, beauty or ideal love.

3) Exhibitionism: The person requires constant attention and admiration.

4) Cool indifference or marked feelings of rage, inferiority, shame, humiliation, or emptiness in response to criticism, indifference of others, or defeat.[16]

A diagnosis of NPD also required at least two of the following issues were present in at least one interpersonal relationship:

1) entitlement: expectation of special favors without assuming reciprocal responsibilities; e.g., surprise and anger that people will not do what is wanted

2) interpersonal exploitativeness: taking advantage of others to indulge own desires or for self-aggrandizement; disregard for the personal integrity and rights of others; relationships that characteristically alternate between the extremes of over idealization and devaluation;

3) Lack of empathy: inability to recognize how others feel; e.g., unable to appreciate the distress of someone who is seriously ill.

The DSM-IV, which offered detailed descriptions of 297 disorders, was published in 1994. The structure of DSM-III remained.[15] Perhaps the most important change introduced by the DSM-IV was a marked increase in reliability. Another important change was the removal of exclusion criteria across several diagnoses. In previous editions of the DSM, exclusion criteria served to lead to a single diagnosis.[15] Multiple diagnoses are a fact of life in clinical psychology and narcissism is no different. For example, many patients with NPD experience both anxiety and depression. Alcoholism and attention problems are also common co-existing conditions. Diagnosing one specific condition should not necessarily eliminate another.

In revising criteria for NPD, the DSM-IV, details were added to better distinguish between NPD and other personality disorders with similar symptoms. For one, the criterion "Cool indifference or marked feelings of rage, inferiority, shame, humiliation, or emptiness in response to criticism, indifference of others, or defeat "was eliminated because it also occurs in other personality disorders, such as Borderline Personality Disorder and Bipolar Disorder, even when other narcissistic traits are not present. Also eliminated was "Exhibitionism: The person requires constant attention and admiration" because the authors believed this criterion implied an overt insecurity that is not immediately apparent in most people with NPD.

Additions to the criteria served to paint a clearer picture of NPD. "Arrogant, haughty behaviors or attitudes" was added to distinguish NPD from personality disorders associated with neediness. "Is often envious of others or believes that others are envious of him or her" was also added. It is common for a narcissist to deal with his own envious feelings by inferring envy of himself on others. The changes served to stress overt characteristics of NPD, such as arrogance, aggressive tendency, self-absorption, and lack of empathy. However, it failed to describe covert experiences of narcissism, such as shame, embarrassment and hyper-vigilance. People with NPD are very sensitive and easily hurt by the reactions of others. Additionally, many people with NPD are aware that they have feelings that are unusually selfish or cold. They struggle with an awareness of how they want to be while also recognizing their natural tendencies.

1) In 2013, the DSM-5 was published, offering the most conceptual changes since the DSM-III.[15] Although still controversial, the changes in DSM-5 were intended to improve diagnostic stability, reliability and validity. This resulted in conceptual changes to several disorders.[17] The five Axis system, which served to categorize disorders, has been removed entirely, and personality disorder clusters have also been eliminated. The DSM-5 now classifies personality disorders, which were classified as Axis II disorders under DSM-IV in the same way

it classifies all other disorders.[15] This means that there is no boundary that categorically separates personality disorders from other disorders, such as depression or autism. Interestingly, during the development of the DSM-5, there was talk—even heated debate—about removing the disorder altogether. The truth is that not everyone, including psychiatrists, agrees that being self-centered is a disorder. After a 2011 revision was published on the APA's website, clinicians petitioned to have NPD included in the latest edition. The current requirements for NPD, as of May, 2013 are as follows:

Significant impairments in personality functioning manifest by:

1) Impairments in self functioning (a *or* b):

   a) Identity: Excessive reference to others for self-definition and self-esteem regulation; exaggerated self-appraisal may be inflated or deflated, or vacillate between extremes; emotional regulation mirrors fluctuations in self-esteem.

   b) Self-direction: Goal-setting is based on gaining approval from others; personal standards are unreasonably high in order to see oneself as exceptional, or too low based on a sense of entitlement; often unaware of own motivations.

   AND

Impairments in interpersonal functioning (a or b):

   a) Empathy: Impaired ability to recognize or identify with the feelings and needs of others; excessively attuned to reactions of others, but only if perceived as relevant to self; over- or underestimate of own effect on others.

   b) Intimacy: Relationships largely superficial and exist to serve self-esteem regulation; mutuality constrained by little genuine interest in others' experiences and predominance of a need for personal gain

      1. Pathological personality traits in the following domain:

A. Antagonism, characterized by:

  (a) Grandiosity: Feelings of entitlement, either overt or covert; self-centeredness; firmly holding to the belief that one is better than others; condescending toward others.

  (b) Attention seeking: Excessive attempts to attract and be the focus of the attention of others; admiration seeking.

  2. The impairments in personality functioning and the individual's personality trait expression are relatively stable across time and consistent across situations.

  3. The impairments in personality functioning and the individual's personality trait expression are not better understood as normative for the individual's developmental stage or socio-cultural environment.

  4. The impairments in personality functioning and the individual's personality trait expression are not solely due to the direct physiological effects of a substance (e.g., a drug of abuse, medication) or a general medical condition (e.g., severe head trauma)[17]

Measurement of NPD and Narcissistic Traits

Since the 1980s, the Narcissistic Personality Inventory (NPI) has been the most common psychometric tool for assessing narcissistic traits. The NPI consists of 40 paired questions, such as "I have a natural talent for influencing people" and "compliments embarrass me." The NPI does not diagnose NPD, but instead measures authority, self-sufficiency, exhibitionism, exploitativeness, vanity, and entitlement. A score between 12 and 15 is average, and a higher score indicates an elevation in one of the tested domains. If an individual has a higher-than-average score, he or she may have narcissistic personality disorder, but a full clinical interview and patient history is necessary to make a diagnosis. Other measures of narcissism exist, but the majority of studies covered in this book used the NPI to determine narcissistic traits in test subjects.

The Future of NPD Research

The history books are not yet closed on NPD. Narcissism is particularly interesting to clinicians and researchers, because it seems to be increasingly common in modern culture. Lack of empathy is a feature of NPD that dates back to Walder's 1925 case study and has been included in every revision of the DSM. Current research has found that changes have occurred in empathy over time, based on changing sociocultural norms. Other traits associated with the narcissistic personality, such as positive self-views, self-promotion, need for approval, materialism, and entitlement are also on the rise. Increased access to the Internet and social networking has led to an increase in social isolation in the real world. This book will examine these changes across several aspects of modern life and will aim to predict the impact a rise in narcissistic traits has on individuals, relationships, families, religion and the media.

Part 2

A NARCISSISTIC CULTURE

Chapter 3

THE NEW NORMAL:
IS IT PATHOLOGY IF EVERYONE
IS DOING IT?

"There comes a time when you look into the mirror and you realize that what you see is all that you will ever be. And then you accept it. Or you kill yourself. Or you stop looking in mirrors."

– Tennessee Williams

"If you spend your life sparing people's feelings and feeding their vanity, you get so you can't distinguish what should be respected in them."

– F. Scott Fitzgerald, *Tender is the Night & The Last Tycoon*

China has a problem. In 1979, amid a faltering economy and unmanageable population, the communist government enacted a strict one-child policy. Although some exceptions have been made, for example twins are allowed, rural families whose first child is a girl may have a second child, and wealthy families willing to pay a fee as much as ten times an average household income may have additional children; the policy is ruthlessly enforced. According to a 2013 article published in the *New York Times* "Village family-planning officers vigilantly chart the menstrual cycle and pelvic-exam results of every woman of childbearing age in their area. If a woman gets pregnant without permission and is unable to pay the often exorbitant fine for violating the policy, she risks being subjected to a forced abortion."[18]

More than half of all Chinese women have had at least one abortion during their lifetime. It is estimated that most procedures are forced, and not a result of maternal choice. Most accounts of forced abortions include being ambushed by city officials, and forced to undergo painful medical procedures without pain management or antibiotics. Women are sent home—many on foot—without follow-up from a doctor. Infection, injury and even death are not uncommon in low-income communities.

Social Changes as a Result of the One Child Policy

China's one-child policy has resulted in a myriad of social changes. As anticipated, the birth rate is down, much lower than the repopulation rate. They also must have anticipated a badly skewed gender gap. Ultrasound technology became available shortly after the policy was enacted, and middle class families had the option to electively abort. Today, China has 122 boys for every 100 girls. It is estimated that by 2020, men will outnumber women by 35 million. These men, who outnumber the entire population of Australia, cannot ever date or marry because enough women simply do not exist.[19] Another problem that may have been anticipated is a growing elderly population without the resources to support them.[18]

However, China never anticipated the changes that would occur to the personalities and cultural values of a generation of singleton children, primarily boys. Studies that date back to 1980 have described Chinese only children as selfish, untrusting, untrustworthy, unsociable, self-centered, risk-averse, pessimistic, insensitive, fragile and cowardly[21], [20] and that they "[make] demands for immediate gratification of their wishes, [display] disrespect for elders, and [have] outbursts of temper."[21] The increase in these characteristics has resulted in a phenomenon known as *little emperor syndrome.* Although Chinese singletons boast higher academic achievements in all subjects compared to their peers with siblings, these little emperors are more likely to be less cooperative and less helpful, and do what they want rather than engage in group activities.[20] Additionally, thanks to a changing economic environment, growing personal freedoms and increased social and developmental opportunities, a 2006 report found that young Chinese people "have a strong interest in self-indulgence and personal entertainment and tend to hold materialistic values."[22]

Differences between only children and children with siblings exist in all cultures. Parents of only children tend to be more responsive to the needs of their children, have more attention to pay and interact more often and with higher quality. At the same time, the parents of only children across cultures tend to have higher expectations and place more pressure for success on their children than parents of two or more children.[20] Although the sibling experience has been found to foster cooperation and empathy in children, only children in other cultures, such as those growing up in the United States do not face the same personality challenges as Chinese singletons because we live in a largely family-friendly culture. If you are an only child living in the United States, you probably have cousins or have friends who have brothers and sisters. Throughout childhood, you will have ample opportunities to observe sibling reactions and interact with children of different ages outside a classroom. Imagine being an only child in a sea of only children. The experience is completely different.

One challenge of understanding the effects of singleton childhoods among the little emperors is that there are very few children with siblings with whom to compare personality traits and behaviors. For example, a study conducted in Beijing found that, in 1975, four years before the one-child policy began, 27% of children born in China had no siblings. By 1983, only four years after the policy began, 90.7% of new babies were only children.[20] As explained earlier, families are permitted to have multiple children only under certain circumstances. Therefore, the family life of singletons is not comparable to that of multiples. The best way to understand the ways that little emperors are unique, while controlling for other factors, is to compare them with Chinese children born before the policy.

One study that successfully compared the characteristics of people born around the same time in China was published in 2013. The study examined several personality traits in men and women born both before and after the policy change. The participants engaged in several activities to measure their levels of altruism, trust, trustworthiness, risk-taking, and competitiveness. As expected, participants born after the one-child policy scored significantly lower on every measure. Participants also took a Big Five Personality Inventory survey. This personality measure asks questions to assess most known personality traits across five categories (openness, conscientiousness, extraversion, agreeableness, and neuroticism). Once again, the participants born after the one-child policy had considerably higher scores in neuroticism and lower in both conscientiousness and optimism.[20]

Understanding Collective Change

China's problem is important to understand, because it illustrates the many ways in which an entire culture can be affected by a collective rise in negative personality traits. As you've likely noticed, many of the traits associated with little emperor syndrome are consistent with NPD traits. In the United States, we want to believe our growing narcissism is just part of an evolving culture. Unfortunately for China, their evolving culture has created a multitude of problems that will not be easily solved. At the Chinese People's Political Consultative Conference in 2007, 30 delegates implored the government to end the one-child policy, stating that it was related to "social problems and personality disorders in young people."[20]

In addition to difficult personality traits, Chinese young people deal with more depression and anxiety than in prior generations. Many grow up their entire lives believing they are their family's *only hope*. Success is almost always attached to education, and young people will stop at nothing to get into the best schools.[23] Suicidal thoughts and behaviors have also increased among young Chinese. A 2008 mental health report found that "pressure to do well in school and feelings of isolation and loneliness are among the main reasons why Chinese high school students consider suicide."[22] Because they have no siblings to share the burden, adults are solely responsible for the care of aging parents. Many couples face the challenge of caring for as many as four elderly parents while raising their own child.[23] Because of these issues and more, it is reasonable to believe that the one-child policy is on its way out. History will likely remember the one-child policy as one of the largest political mistakes in world history, and one that did permanent damage to generations of citizens. Most importantly, we may learn that ignoring a problem will not make it go away.

Increasing Narcissism, Decreasing Empathy

Every generation seems to think their own is the best. The older generation is out of touch, and the younger is immature, selfish and lazy all because they missed out on the *good ol' days*. This world view is necessary for a sense of self-preservation, continuing innovation and to make sure that beliefs and ideas are passed on to the new generation. Just ask your grandmother, this is not new. However, the understanding that young people are more narcissistic than ever before is not an imagined notion, or the rant of an older generation. In the same way that sociologists and psychologists became concerned about the choices made by the Chinese government decades before the damage was clear; experts have been concerned about narcissism among the millennial generation for some time. The millennial generation, also known as Y, is made up of people born between 1980 and 2000. Real evidence and compelling statistics show an increase in narcissism and a decrease in empathy in the current generation.

A meta-analysis of 85 samples of American college students between 1982 and 2006 found a significant increase in narcissist traits.[24] America, as a culture, is also becoming more narcissistic. Studies that aim to evaluate the perception of national culture (PNC) have revealed that the PNC of the United States leads the 40 countries examined in narcissistic traits such as self-esteem, agreeability, and extroversion. These findings suggest that the rise in individual narcissistic traits has resulted in a culture that is both experienced and perceived as narcissistic.[25]

As discussed in Chapters 1 and 2, a lack of empathy, now qualified as an "impaired ability to recognize or identify with the feelings and needs of others; excessively attuned to reactions of others, but only if perceived as relevant to self; over- or underestimate of own effect on others" has been an important aspect of the narcissistic personality since it was first conceptualized, and has remained through every stage of revision, research and study. Although NPD requires a pathological level of several aspects of disordered thinking and behavior, a cultural pattern of decreased empathy creates cause for concern. Empathy is an important part of the human experience that transcends culture. Empathy is necessary for cooperation and relating to others, and facilitates relationships on both a personal and community level. The specific definition of empathy varies, depending on who you ask, but it typically refers to a cognitive or affective construct of understanding the feelings of others and reacting to the experience of others.[26]

Some research has proposed that today's young generation is more empathetic than previous generations. A 2008 study of 2,000 young adults classified as the "millennial generation" found that this generation—who drive hybrid cars, occupy Wall Street, and buy canvas shoes so that identical shoes can be donated to children in third world countries—describe themselves in positive terms and view themselves as more empathetic than previous generations. In fact, 90% of participants agreed that their generation is "set apart" from earlier generations. This study was unable to make a convincing argument for the empathy of young adults, and instead supported the belief that they see themselves as special. Is it possible that behaving in a way once aligned with empathy makes people feel better about themselves? Even with a decline in empathy, volunteer work among high school students has risen significantly. Of course, this coincides with high school volunteerism requirements and colleges looking for volunteer experience. Almost all young adults ages 18-25 answered that donating to charity is important, yet they only donate a fraction of what older adults donate to charities and churches, even when the amount is adjusted for income disparities. At the same time that violent crime is declining in the United States, specific types of crimes are increasing. Violence against the homeless population, for example, as well as members of the gay, lesbian and transgender community are at all-time highs. There has also been a sharp rise in violence against Hispanics and other perceived immigrants. A rise in violence against stigmatized, marginalized and defenseless people is indicative of low empathy. Examinations of social trends argue that empathy is not disappearing, but none of these studies have used empirical data, or were successfully able to compare current data with data from older generations.[26]

Most research that has found a rise in narcissistic traits has examined the thoughts and behaviors of college students. In general, the demographics for American college students have not changed much over the years. When adjusted for inflation, the median family income of American undergraduates has increased by less than $3,000 since 1985. Although women and ethnic minorities have more opportunities for higher education than in the past, the increase is not statistically significant. An analysis of 72 studies that examined empathy in college students between 1979 and 2009 found a very real decline in empathic traits. Modern college students were less likely to endorse statements such as "I take action to help others even if it does not personally benefit me," and "I try to imagine how my friends feel" than their parents' generation did at their same age. In all of the data, spanning more than three decades, women expressed more empathy than men, but there were no differences where ethnicity or socioeconomic status was considered.[26]

Why is Narcissism Increasing?

As you can imagine, the reasons for an increase in narcissism and decline in empathy are controversial. Just like gun control, or access to violent video games, the answers depend on who you ask. Changes in media content and usage are a popular culprit. Even if everyone agreed that changes in media are problematic, this would not prove that media causes changes in empathy and other narcissistic traits. Changes in social norms could also lead to changes in media reflective of culture. Social media sites, such as Facebook and Twitter are an unprecedented trend and phone usage is higher than during any other time. Teens have enjoyed talking on the phone for generations, but the introduction of text messaging, games and mobile social networking have created higher interest and more opportunities than in generations past. Television use is more prevalent, and the average household owns 4 televisions, and multiple computers. The average American experiences a 350% increase in total daily information, outside of work or school than 30 years ago.

Because young people today have so many opportunities to see hurt, violence, war, poverty, and terrorism in the media, it is likely that they become desensitized and no longer understand the horror of true human suffering. No matter what you believe, it is obvious that these social changes have affected the individual in *some way*, even if that way is unclear. One hypothesis is the changes in the way we interact equate to a change in social skills, primarily empathy. People rely less on social gatherings and family dinners, and more on the instant feedback of peers. The relative speed of online communication may have also led to boredom, frustration and less patience.[26]

Parenting style is another possible cause for decrease in empathy. Although no correlation has been found between parental empathy and a child's empathy, parents with a non-authoritarian disciplinary style, and who are generally warm and patient tend to raise more empathic children. Shrinking family size may also contribute. As we have learned from the China crisis, the sibling experience is an important part of developing social skills both related and unrelated to empathy, such as conflict-resolution, taking turns, and playing with others instead of watching television or playing video games alone.[26]

Another possibility is that increasing narcissism reflects a changing set of American values. The majority of 18-25 year old participants in a 2006 survey said that getting rich was among the most important goals for their generation. Less than a third said it was important to help those in need. Reality television may also reflect changing values. Because "ordinary" people are poised to be the stars of reality television shows, they are often more narcissistic than the average person. Every reality program, from Survivor in 2000, to Keeping up With the Kardashians, which is still going strong in 2013, contains characters who believe they are somehow superior to others. Competition shows, with themes ranging from cooking to makeup artistry, focus on a single winner amid multiple losers, a formula consistent with decreasing empathy and a focus on personal success.[26]

Winning the Trophy without Playing the Game

When my son was 11 years old, he broke his arm during soccer practice only a week into the season. To avoid further injury, he was unable to practice or play any games for the remainder of the season. Around the time his team was competing in the play-off games, we received an email inviting us to the team pizza party. The team mom noted that my son should attend to receive his trophy. In their article entitled "Unadulterated Arrogance: Autopsy of the Narcissistic Parental Alienator," Summers and Summers explain the difference between narcissism and self-esteem. "Bona fide self-esteem comes from true accomplishment and being true to one's self. Narcissistic entitlement does not return respect—rather it wants the "trophy" without playing the game."[27] Although this is a metaphor for a mindset, we live in a time where children are quite literally given trophies without needing to play the game.

Today's trophy generation is characterized as lazy and entitled. A May 2013 article in *Time Magazine* reported that 40% of millennials believe they should be promoted every two years, regardless of job performance and that more young people live with their parents further into adulthood than during any previous generation.[28] Every generation of parents has wanted to raise happy, healthy kids. What did the parents of Generation Y do that turned out so wrong? One possibility is that the definitions of happiness and success have changed. Being comfortable and content is no longer good enough. Now happiness means winning and being the best at all times, even though it is unclear exactly at what Generation Y is best.

Welcome to the Self-Esteem Generation

Another possibility is a societal shift to focusing on the self-esteem of children. I can remember when the self-esteem movement began across schools and parenting lore in the United States because I remember my mother complaining about it. "Kids don't need to learn self-esteem" she would complain, "They need to learn to read and write." I thought she was out of touch, of course. This was a time when quips such as "you can do anything you put your mind to" and "you are special" rang out across every school in the country. Who wouldn't want self-esteem? How could it be bad to feel good about yourself, your worth, and your potential? It turns out that my mother was right, and an entire generation of feel-good propaganda was wrong. Initially, the inclusion of self-esteem in schools made sense.

Think back to 1954, when segregation in schools had been the norm throughout the South. When the Supreme Court ruled in Brown vs. The Board of Education, they stated "to separate [children] from others of similar age and qualifications solely because of their race generates a feeling of inferiority as to their status in the community that may affect their hearts and minds in a way unlikely ever to be undone."[29] They were right, of course. Segregation took a devastating emotional and intellectual toll on its victims, and this dark part of history should not be taken lightly. The educational disparity between minority children and white children is no myth. Research throughout the 1980s and 1990s also found a steady relationship between low self-esteem and conduct problems among school children. It was found that children with low self-esteem may cope with negative feelings by acting out, which may lead to developing relationships with deviant peers. Because low socio-economic status is also linked to low self-esteem, it seemed logical that raising self-esteem would also improve school performance and classroom behavior.[30] The problem was that these changes were made based on shallow knowledge of self-esteem and how to raise it.

Before the 1980s were over, self-esteem was a popular part of curriculum. Author Maureen Stout describes the result of this shift as "transform[ing] schools into therapeutic clinics and teachers into counselors, creating a generation of entitled, righteous, underachieving children."[31] The movement has produced a generation with a very *shallow* sense of self-esteem, based on a perceived self-worth unrelated to accomplishments.

One explanation as to why this occurred is that opposed to true self-esteem, which is characterized as a person thinking well of himself, the narcissistic self-esteem produced through feel-good curriculum is a *motivational* construct, characterized as a *desire* to think well of oneself and an expectation that others share this view.[30] Instead of a sense of pride developed through hard work, talent and accomplishment, children of the post-self-esteem movement believe they *must* be successful because they want to be, and others should respect their desires. Another problem is that when children expect something to be easy and it is difficult, they give up and do not try. In Chapter 1, we discussed symptoms of childhood narcissism. Among the signs was a tendency to give up on challenging activities. Unfortunately, this is becoming increasingly common among children who are told that everything they do is brilliant. When they think there is a possibility of failure, they simply give up.

The Self-Esteem Myth

One of the ways the self-esteem movement erred is that it put praise before accomplishment, not the other way around. Like the earlier example about earning trophies without playing the game, students are being praised without having to earn it. The theory behind this practice is that praise is a strong motivator. *If a child believes she is brilliant, she will behave as though she is brilliant.* Stout identified several myths related to self-esteem in education, and many problems associated with Generation Y seem to come directly from this list. For one, the first myth states that, "High expectations for students are damaging to their self-esteem."[31] On the contrary, a teacher with high expectations will motivate students to make an effort and risk failure. When praise comes at the end, the student is being rewarded for what he really did accomplish, whether the accomplishment is dedication or true goal achievement.

Two other myths identified by Stout are "Discipline is bad for self esteem and should be dispensed with" and "It is the teacher's, not the student's responsibility to ensure learning."[31] Don't get me wrong, I am thankful that the days of shaming and physical discipline in schools are long gone. But somehow, natural consequences for both bad behavior and poor academic performance have also disappeared. In many high schools, red pens are no longer used for correcting papers, because the highly visible markings make students feel bad about their work. Teachers are also called to take responsibility when their students perform poorly. Districts across the country are called to evaluate teacher performance based on standardized test scores, with no consideration of the study habits or home life of students. In an informational packet purported to raise self-esteem, teacher are instructed to "remove the threat of failure: say, "This is very hard, but don't worry if you find it difficult. It's my fault for giving you such hard work" and "Take the blame for failure: say, 'I'm sorry I didn't explain that properly. It's my fault. Let me try again.'"[31] When it comes down to it, failure is no longer an option in school.

The Self-Esteem Movement at Home

The popular self-esteem movement, that re-trained teachers as therapists, has also found its way into parenting books and average American homes. Most parents have come to believe that praising children is necessary for building self-esteem. Current research has found that too much praise is actually harmful for children. A 2013 Stanford University study found that children who were praised for effort (*"I love the colors you chose for your painting"*) rather than personally (*"You are such a great artist!"*) had higher self-esteem and were better able to make changes and adapt than children who were praised personally.[32] This information is not new.

One of my favorite parenting books, written by Dr. Haim G. Ginott in 1965 includes an entire chapter on praising children. Dr. Ginott explained that our words are only one part of praise, and that the child's inference of the praise is the more important element. "Our words should state clearly that we appreciate the child's effort, work, achievement, help consideration, or creation. Our words should be framed that the child will almost inevitably draw from them a realistic conclusion about his personality."[33] This is realistic advice.

Consider your own self-esteem and the way you perceive your own strengths and weaknesses. How closely are they linked to the direct praise of others? Likely, the inferences you have made from the feedback of others is more closely linked to your self-image. So, why has an entire generation of parents ignored the work of experts and instead chose to heap unconstructive praise onto children? The most likely explanation is social pressure. When parents hear other people tell their children then are so smart, so talented, and so beautiful, they worry that their children will feel badly about themselves if they do not follow suit. In fact, many of the counter-productive choices that parents make are based on fear of being bad parents. *If my child is playing outside unsupervised , wearing mismatched clothes, or behaving like a child I am a bad parent.*

I understand first-hand how it feels to be pressured as a parent. When my older son was about three years old, he loved jumping across rocks. He did this every morning as we walked back from taking his older sister to school. Every morning, he would say, "I bet you think I can't jump across this!" And sometimes he would request that I *tell* him that he could not jump from one place to another. Of course I knew what was going on. Defying expectations of what a little boy could do made him feel proud. If he believed I thought he couldn't do something and he proved me wrong, that made him shockingly strong and capable. Even though my child was essentially *telling me* what he needed to develop a healthy sense of self-esteem I was so inundated by false self-esteem culture, that I was afraid of damaging his self-esteem. Even more, I was worried that another parent would overhear and think I was damaging my child's self-esteem!

Difficulty Establishing Authority

Today's parents also seem to have a difficult time establishing authority. My own children attend a lovely Waldorf school in southern California. Waldorf education does a beautiful job of educating the whole child, but soon after my oldest child began attending, I noticed that the teachers use very peculiar language when addressing the pupils. Instead of using direct language to communicate instructions, they begin all requests with "you may." *You may come…John may pay attention…Sarah may sit quietly.* And when a child is caught behaving badly, the typical teacher response is a swift "no thank you." Before long, parents on the playground were using the same language, but without a standard of classroom management techniques in play, they were not getting the same results. "Tyler, you may come," said one frustrated mother. Before long, she was barking the request, with a tone that could have said, "get over here right now!" Eventually, she had to remove her child from the park physically. This is a pattern seen at playgrounds around the country. Parents afraid to establish gentle but firm authority plead with their kids to behave and then get frustrated and assert an inappropriate level of tyranny. I do not know why this particular school uses a special type of speech when relating to children. After reading Waldorf curriculum books and talking to teachers, I did not get a straight answer. However, I can speculate that avoiding direct contact is a way to avoid discipline, and more importantly, it is a gentler method than straight-talk. Both of these possibilities are marked as areas of concern by Stout. First, that discipline has no place in school, and second, that a teacher should be a friend. Another possibility is that by hearing the words "you may" before a reprimand or correction, the child feels a sense of empowerment. If they *may* do it, it is their choice and they have control over their behavior. I have been unable to find any information or research to indicate that this method is used in other schools, or that there is evidence that it is useful. In the absence of any evidence, I can surmise that like other feel-good curriculum, aimed at raising self-esteem, it will disrupt the natural and necessary authority that parents need to have.

Again, I advocate for fairness and flexibility in parenting and teaching. Children should be treated with respect, and I cringe whenever I hear a parent say, *get over here right now!* The problem is that when authority is not established or maintained, the child takes on emotional responsibilities outside of his developmental capabilities, creating a shallow, false self-esteem. Another problem with establishing authority comes when a parent gives their children inappropriate choices. *Do you want to eat now?* (When it is dinner time), *Do you want to sit in your car seat* (When the family is about to pull out of the driveway), *Do you want to go home?* (When the parent has to be home in twenty minutes) are inappropriate questions because only one answer will do. When the child makes the wrong choice, the parent must intervene with a level of authority that does not match the choice. A similar problem occurs when a parent, ready to leave the playground says, "goodbye, I'm leaving" and walks away as though abandoning the child. In this case, the parent is giving the child a false empowerment, and a fake choice. He must wrestle with making the choice to leave an activity or risk abandonment. Before long, he realizes his parents *won't* abandon him and authority is lost again.

Royal Babies and Rock Stars

My family visits the Los Angeles County Fair every fall. One year, when my daughter was three years old, the children's building featured a display sponsored by the Los Angeles Fire Department. The display taught families important information about fire safety, and at the end, children could dress up in real fire fighter uniforms. I can't remember the exact circumstances, but a very kind fireman called my daughter "princess." "I'm not a princess", she corrected, and he replied, still smiling "To me you are a princess." Frustrated, my daughter tried one more time "No, I mean my mom and dad are not a king and queen." Somewhere along the line, calling our daughters "princess" has become routine, and even expected. At first, this trend bothered me because of the gender stereotypes associated with it. For example, a friend recently posted on Facebook that she was excited about the niece she was expecting. She explained that she *knew* the little girl would be a *princess* and that her own son would be eager protect her. How could she possibly know this about an unborn baby or her toddler son who probably wasn't interested in protecting anything but his own toys? Although assigning gender roles to infants bothers me on a personal and sociological level, the real problem with the *princess* epidemic is that implies that ordinary little girls are somehow special and entitled to be regarded as royalty.

American parents don't just tell their kids they are special, they tell the whole world. Parents can post pictures of their children to social networking sites, along with their own hashtags. If your child says something adorable, make sure to post the entire dialogue on Facebook, along with their excellent grades, the outcome of parent-teacher conferences and a photo of their most recent test. Video uploading websites like YouTube are full of videos of cute children doing cute and not-so-cute things. If your child does something crazy enough, he may just get his fifteen minutes of fame before he can walk. Sayings on t-shirts are now the norm, and it is difficult to find infant clothes that do not advertise "princess" or "rock star."

The Bubble Wrapped Childhood

When modern parents aren't praising their children (for virtually nothing), they are bubble wrapping their childhoods in an attempt to prevent failure and hurt feelings. I recently watched a home video of a friend's grandson meeting Mickey Mouse during a recent visit to Disneyworld. As the excited toddler approaches his favorite character, the mother's voice, off-screen says "say hi, Mickey!" The little boy repeats *Hi Mickey!* Moments later the mother instructs "give Mickey a kiss!...say goodbye, Mickey!" Before the little boy can remove his arms from the mouse's neck, another instruction sings "say thank you, Mickey!" And just like that, what is likely the most exciting moment of the two-year-old boy's life has been scripted, directed and executed before he had an opportunity to enjoy it. This is a prime example of a well-meaning parent so invested in her child's development that she is eager to remove any discomfort, disappointment or possible bad manners from a fun encounter. The same situations play out at every rubber-cushioned playground in the country. Parents stand by, armed with sanitizing hand gel, ready to coach their children in how to play with others.[34]

Changing Childhood Play

For most of history, play was an important component of childhood learning. Today, 40,000 schools in the United States have removed recess from their daily schedule, and fear of kidnappers keep children indoors instead of playing in their neighborhoods. Organized sports offer an opportunity for outdoor play, but are typically managed and closely monitored by adults. Even spontaneous, free-play between children has all but disappeared. Now, if two children want to play, they must ask their parent to arrange a "play date." This language is completely normalized among parents and children, but represents a serious shift in the way children learn to relate to others and develop a sense of self. Free, unsupervised play is necessary for cognitive agility, decision-making, leadership skills, memory and mental processing skills.

My Child is Too Good to Catch an Infectious Disease

At the same time parents are becoming increasingly germaphobic, another interesting trend is that modern parents are now refusing to vaccinate their children against dangerous infectious disease. There are a variety of reasons for this decision—ranging from religious beliefs, to fear of autism. My friend, Maura explained "I don't necessarily think my kids won't get sick, but I would prefer them to actually get sick and gain immunity naturally rather than get the vaccine." In any case, the trend has become so popular that health officials across several states worry about outbreaks of diseases that were at one time eradicated, such as measles and whooping cough. In the United States, parents have the right to not vaccinate for personal reasons, but an ethical dilemma exists surrounding who is responsible when a child becomes sick. Children under a year old, for example, are too young to be vaccinated, yet they can become infected when exposed to a sick child whose parents made the decision to not vaccinate. A 2012 article in the *Journal of Law, Medicine & Ethics* stated, "One can make a legitimate, state-sanctioned choice not to vaccinate, but that does not protect the person making that choice against the consequences of that choice for others."[35]

Choosing not to vaccinate one's children does not make the parent a narcissist in and of itself, but the idea that one's child won't get an infectious disease *is* a narcissistic position. Pediatrician Michelle Au addressed this issue in *Psychology Today*:

> I see people who are not only rejecting what we have to offer, but are *vilifying* doctors and other healthcare workers—who have devoted decades of their lives to caring for children and families and continue to work their hardest to give patients the highest quality care we know how. And quite frankly, it hurts my feelings. It's not just paternalism, it's not about me wanting to tell patients what to do and for them to comply mindlessly, it's about me wanting to do my job and

do it well, always, for everyone. And when I feel like people reject my efforts and recast my motives as somehow <u>evil</u>, greedy, or just plain ignorant, *it hurts my feelings.*[36]

It's easy to see where this position comes from. Today's new parents are almost exclusively from Generation X and Generation Y. This generation grew up being weary of profit-hungry pharmaceutical companies, and with Internet savvy that makes us believe we know as much as medical professionals. This generation also grew up in a time of immunization, when chicken pox was a childhood rite of passage, not the deadly disease it was a generation before. Most new parents today never had a childhood friend crippled as a result of polio or die from measles. This bubble of privilege makes us feel safe, as though infectious diseases are an antiquated problem, not a reality threatening to kill children.

We are also afraid of doing or saying anything that will make our children feel bad. A few years ago, a friend's husband was telling me about the garden he had planted with his two pre-school aged sons. "We are growing tomatoes, zucchini, corn and spinach," he explained. His wife seemed surprised, and commented, "I didn't know we were growing spinach, I thought that was chard." He quickly replied, "The boys don't know what chard is, so we call it spinach." This father clearly isn't lazy—he enjoys spending his free time gardening with his children and *wants* them to learn about the world. So, what would make a parent not want to explain something like the name of a vegetable to their child? Kids learn new things every day. Like many parents, this father didn't want his sons to have a moment of the discomfort that comes with not understanding something new.

Competitive Parents,
Competitive Children

When my youngest son was a baby, the latest in a string of products aimed to turn ordinary babies into geniuses was unveiled. Called "Your Baby Can Read," the set of DVDs promises that for only $200, your baby will learn to read...and when he masters that, he can read in foreign languages, too. Never mind that your baby would eventually learn to read without the help of expensive videos. There is nothing *special* about a school-aged child who can read. Today, new parents put iPads in front of their infants, and many babies can effectively tap and swipe before their first birthdays. In a small study sponsored by *ABC News*, infants and toddlers chose tablets over their mothers when presented with both. The American Academy of Pediatrics has, for years, been clear that any screen time for children under two of age is not recommended.[37] Yes, even seemingly harmless shows like Sesame Street are not helpful to very young children. Because the technology is new, no studies have examined the real harm done by tablets but years of research has found time and time again that not only does educational programming not help children under two learn, parents consistently overestimate the benefit. One study asked a group of parents to have their 12-18 month old baby watch a Baby Einstein video alone every day for one month. Another group of infants watched the video with a parent, and a third group did not watch the video. At the end of the month, the parents in both video groups had a higher estimate of what their children learned, but the children in the no-media group had a much larger increase in vocabulary during the same period. In fact, even the babies of most confident parents in the media group showed less change than the babies in the media-free group. One reason that parents over-estimate the benefit of media in learning is that children naturally increase vocabulary and when a child is exposed to many forms of language; it is difficult to determine which made the difference.[38]

The studies done today on children and media exposure are not breaking news. Still, parents continue to believe that there is some benefit. One of the reasons has a lot to do with competition and wanting our children to be the best and the smartest. My friend Mandy has two daughters who both spoke very early and developed strong vocabularies and mathematical abilities at a young age. She was young and poor when she had her first child, and they didn't have a radio in their car. She and her then-toddler would pass the time counting aloud together and saying the alphabet. She recalls that they counted into the 100s and that those interactions helped her daughter develop a strong foundation for learning. Now, 15 years later, Mandy is raising another toddler, and this time with the help of a tablet, although, unlike many parents, she only uses it a few times every week and always while she is in the room with her child. When I asked her why she uses it, she said "I honestly would not know all of the things she needs to be learning at different stages or how to teach her these things." If a mom, like Mandy, who is doing a great job teaching her children, worries that they won't learn what they *should* learn, I imagine that parents whose children struggle, or are behind schedule would be even more anxious.

Parents aren't the only ones trying to boost learning with technology. The Los Angeles Unified School District (LAUSD) has dealt with failures across several areas for years, and thought they could "catch up" by outfitting every student in the district with an iPad for the 2013 school year (nothing else has worked—technology must be what's missing!) Believe it or not, problems starting cropping up before the ink on the $1 billion check had dried. More than 300 tech-savvy kids had hacked into the school's security system designed to keep students out of social networking sites within days. About a week after the program started, 70 iPads (read: $47,000) had gone missing. In another district with a similar program, children were robbed walking home from school, and some parents sold the devices for money. So far, no actual learning from the project has occurred. Other snags included Wi-Fi going down, leaving kids unable to complete assignments on time;[39] and despite the high cost of brand name tablets, frustrated teachers are still required to take as many as a dozen unpaid days off each year.

The need to compete doesn't stop in childhood. As many as 30% of college students have used "study drugs" commonly prescribed for attention deficit hyperactivity disorder (ADHD) to help with focus and drive when studying for a big test. ADHD drugs are easier to get than marijuana, and particularly popular in competitive schools, where students feel more pressure to meet demands. Steroid use among athletes has come to the forefront, as popular and successful baseball players, football players, cyclists, body builders and Olympic athletes have used them to gain a competitive advantage. All of these people were good at what they did to begin with, but the need to be *the best* drove them to make poor decisions at a high cost. In addition to risking credibility and careers, the physical and psychological side of effects of popular performance-enhancing drugs includes acne, headaches, vision problems, hair loss, kidney and liver disease, pain, swelling, tremors, prostate problems, depression, hallucination and aggressive behavior.

As badly as parents want their children to win, they want to make sure they never feel the discomfort of losing. In October 2013, a high school football team in Texas lost a game. They lost, and lost badly—91 to 0! The coach of the winning team says that after he realized how steeply his team would win, he tried to level the playing field by letting the clock run and instructing his players to not pass the ball. Still, an angry parent filed a formal complaint, claiming that the losing team was bullied. That's right, bullied! There was no violence, no threats, not even playful teasing. The angry father said in his complaint that he didn't know what to say to his son on the tough ride home. Instead of telling him that losing is part of life, or that he loves him whether he wins or loses, his natural response was to file a complaint and accuse a coach who was doing his job, of bullying.

How Did We Let This Happen?

Generation Y children are typically the offspring of Boomers and Generation X, so some logical conclusions can be drawn. They were raised to accept that "because I said so" was a valid parental argument and that if all their friends jumped off a bridge, it certainly didn't mean they should. Their parents sided with teachers—no matter what really happened, and tended to be hands-off in the classroom. Generation X was the first to be raised by working mothers, and divorced parents. They were the first "latch-key" kids. Generation X was the earliest generation inundated by the media, so they were the first to hear about children kidnapped off the street and children to be killed in car accidents. Generation X came of age in a time of science and technology, which means a heightened understanding, and maybe sensitivity to illness and germs!

Again, please don't get me wrong. I'm thankful for new laws and policies that protect children. My own children have been vaccinated and wear helmets when riding bikes (although, I must admit sometimes they don't wear shoes) and we won't pull out of the driveway without car seats and seatbelts safely adjusted and buckled (while I'm still looking for those shoes). The point is that the over-protective nature of the Boomers and Generation X came from a lifetime of hurt feelings and over-evaluation of perceived danger. These generations vowed to never be like their parents and to do things differently. Consider the fear of germs. For example, sometime around the mid-2000s, shopping cart covers became a popular—and expensive—baby accessory. This new nursery essential covers a shopping cart so that a baby can sit in it comfortably and without touching any bacteria. Car seats and bicycle helmets save lives, but shopping cart covers make a generation of insecure adults feel like *good parents*. What's more, today's parents spend 40% less time with their children than the generation before.[40] It's certainly not for lack of caring, but today's parents out-source parenting (music lessons, tutoring, and organized sports) and therefore are not *with* their children. Even being physically present does not make up for increased use of electronics, which often distract parents from engaging with their children.

Leaving our Children Behind

Starting in 2000, American schools underwent changes to curriculum and educational standards. Although the new policies claimed that educational problems stemmed from discrimination, the changes clearly ignored years of sociological research on the connection between schools and discrimination-related inequality. Instead of offering help to under-achieving schools, funds were removed and the jobs of principals and teachers were taken. Additionally, all schools became college-prep academies, with the expectation that all high school graduates would be college-ready. This may sound like a wonderful promise to parents, but the truth is that not all people are cut out for college. Farm and trade-workers are equally important in society and to an economy. These changes created an unfortunate trend. Increased expectations from parents and the government led way to grade inflation. The pressure put on teachers led to cheating. Teachers across the nation have been found to give answers during standardized tests, and even erase wrong answers and correct them after testing hours. Whether from lowered expectations, or outright cheating, grades and test scores improved without improved understanding of material. Accountability lessened, as absences and late work had a lesser effect on grades than in past years.[41] In 2012, 60% of graduating seniors who took the ACT test did not meet standards for at least two of the four benchmarks for college readiness. Only a quarter of test takers met all benchmarks. More than a quarter were unable to meet the minimum score for any portion of the exam.[42] Somehow, more pressure and higher standards are not producing happier or more competent students. Instead of learning to think, children are learning how to seek praise and take tests. Somehow, there is a serious disconnect between the efforts of parents and the expectations of the school system.

How can it be bad to Feel Good?

It's easy to dismiss the feel-good, self-esteem boosting interactions between children and their parents and teachers. Obviously, it isn't abuse. These children are loved and cared for, and from a global perspective, children in our world face bigger problems, like abuse, prostitution, war, food shortages and contaminated water. Why is it important, or even relevant to worry about how parents talk to, help and coach their kids? These trends are of concern because as long as parents and schools are preparing children for an unrealistic world based on false academic achievement and self-esteem, they are missing important developmental markers and joining the adult world unprepared. The well-loved, well cared for children of Generation Y have an unprecedented rate of depression and anxiety during college and most of these problems are directly related to being coddled. Most notably, the pressure for parents to pad their children with self-esteem diminishes their true sense of self, a known contributor to increased narcissistic traits.

Growing Up Too Fast or Not Growing Up at All?

For years, the term *growing up too fast* has been used to describe a variety of social issues involving children. At one time, adults who spent their own childhoods walking miles to school, being responsible for raising siblings, working in fields and watching other children die from preventable diseases wanted to shield their children from *growing up too fast*. A generation later, the term referred to the sexualization of young girls in the media. Sexy dolls, over-sexualized characters on children's programming and lacey underwear sold in child sizes are examples of *growing up too fast*. The term has also been used to describe many of the pressures discussed in this chapter, and it means that children who should be concerned with play are worried about piles of homework, competition and adult-defined success.

More recently, however, parents and psychologists have been worried about the effects of growing up too fast, while simultaneously *not growing up at all.* A 2010 study found that millennials have delayed each of the five milestones classically associated with adulthood: graduating school, moving out of the family home, achieving financial independence, getting married, and having children. In 1960, Three quarters of women and 65% of men had reached all of these milestones before their 30th birthday. By the 2000 census, only half of women and a third of men had met these milestones. Although the economy can be blamed for most of these changes (who can do any of these things when student debt has doubled since Generation X graduated college?), changing values are also at play.

Another factor is that teens today can communicate with peers more often and more efficiently than ever before. Texting makes communication so accessible that talking to adults is almost obsolete. Before high school was the norm, kids talked to their parents and other relatives. Until a decade ago, communication with peers was limited to class breaks, weekends, and occasional afternoon phone calls and visits. Even then, having to talk to an adult was a possibility. When I called my friends' homes or rang the doorbell, there was a good chance an adult would answer and I would have to engage in polite, adult conversation. No need—*text when you get to the door, continue to text throughout dinner with your parents.* This stunts intellectual growth, development and maturation, as teens are not relating to or learning from adults the way they did in the past.

For better or for worse, what millennials want out of adulthood is different than what previous generations wanted. Only slightly more than 10% of young people want to own a home at some point, a sharp contrast to the American dream of past generations. The average young adult goes through seven jobs during his or her twenties. Of course, there are positive aspects of these changes, too. More young adults go to college than ever before, and women are free to pursue careers and interests outside of motherhood. Although many experts are concerned for the rapid change in societal norms, some are defending this stage of adulthood as a distinct stage of life, similar to adolescence, which was ignored until the early 1900s. These scientists insist that because the brain continues to grow until 25, most young adults are not fully prepared for emotional control and high-order cognitive function. Still, even if delaying adulthood, as it has been previously defined, is healthy and developmentally appropriate, the world outlook of this group of adults is oddly impractical. Amid high unemployment rates, crippling personal and educational debt, and once again living under their parent's roof, 96% of millennials say they are very certain they will eventually get where they want to be in life.[43]

The brains of young adults developed the same fifty years ago as they do today, so it is important to understand that changing cultural norms have a lot to do with these social changes. For one, the self-esteem method of educating and raising children has resulted in adults afraid to take risks, unable to work effectively with others, and with an attitude of entitlement. Before television and print ads, men could go their entire lives without seeing a beautiful woman. Now, most men can't go an hour without seeing one on TV, the Internet, or magazine. Not only are women used to sell products, our society tells men that they *deserve* a beautiful women. The hero of just about every book "gets the girl" at the end, and television characters never date ordinary women. As heroes in our own story, we start to believe that somehow we are entitled, and as societal norms change, the umbrella of this entitlement grows. *Why marry her when someone better will come along? Why take that job when I deserve better? Why shouldn't I go back for another degree when I know I am smarter than most people? Why would I rent an apartment when I could live in my parents' large house?* In short, entitlement (sometimes re-framed as empowerment or self-assuredness) is to blame for the many ways that adulthood is being delayed.

Winning the Blame Game

Sexual assault and physical abuse are not new. Stories of rape and abductions are common in Greek and Roman mythology, as well as Christian and Islamic history. Today, one out of every four women in the United States is a victim of sexual assault at some time during her lifetime. And while years of research have gone into understanding and helping victims, it is only recently that perpetrators have been more closely examined. An online survey conducted in 2010 and 2011 found that two percent of teens and young adults, ages 14 to 21 had completed a rape, but many more admitted to touching someone who did not want to be touched, coerced someone into unwilling sex, or attempted rape. The perpetrators who did not use physical force admitted to getting the victim drunk, using guilt, or arguing with or relentlessly pressuring the victim. Although boys tend to be the perpetrators at a younger age, by 18, girls are just as likely to coerce partners into sex. This survey was the first of its kind, and the results were shocking.

More worrisome than the acts being committed by young people was the deflection of blame. Half of the teens and young adults who admitted to rape or other forms of sexual coercion said that the victim was to blame. Only one third of participants took full responsibility for their behaviors.[44] Like the decrease in empathy among young people, fingers are pointed in several directions when it comes to rise in the prevalence of sexually aggressive behavior. Most experts agree that something needs to change about the way kids are taught about sex. What's more frightening to me is that externalizing blame is increasing at a rate consistent with the decline in empathy and increase in other narcissistic traits. As discussed earlier, deflecting blame is a trait consistent with narcissism. A person with NPD cannot handle any level of shame or guilt, and therefore blames others for behaviors and feelings. The entitled Generation Y feels that they are not to blame for the problems they create.

During the fall of 2011, a new movement sprang up in New York City. After 700 protesters were arrested on the Brooklyn Bridge, the movement spread to cities and towns across the country and eventually to Athens, Brussels, Paris and other major metropolitan cities around the world. Known as Occupy Wall Street (OWS), and eventually The Occupy Movement, one of the movement's initial concerns was that 99% of the wealth in The United States was controlled by one percent of the population. The rest of the population was then known as "The 99%." OWS protesters—presumably with no jobs—camped in large metropolitan cities and small neighborhoods, refusing to leave until their demands had been met. Protesters across the country were arrested (both fairly and unfairly) and at OWS's first birthday celebration, New York police made another 100 arrests. Unlike other major movements before it, the Occupy movement had no leadership and no concrete cause. Today, a visit to OWS's website shows that branches of the movement have occupied the media, poor neighborhoods, the mortgage industry, education, labor, banks, farms, prisons, and every other institution imaginable.

OWS organizers and protestors had reason to be frustrated. Mostly made of Generation Y-ers, they felt the sting of the recent mortgage crisis, one of the longest recessions in U.S. history, and student loans that were impossible to pay. Nobody blamed OWS for their frustration, but many critiqued their method. Because they had no clear leadership or direction, they appeared scattered, and more of a public nuisance than a solution. By the movement's second birthday in the fall of 2013, not much had changed. At a Manhattan event, celebrating the group's ongoing strength, protestor Cathy O'Neil urged anyone interested to take a free copy of the group's book, promising that it "explains how the systems uses us, how the bankers scam us, how the regulators fail to do their job."[45] This sentiment presents a sharp contrast from the inner-workings of the Tea Party Movement (TPM), a staunchly conservative group established in 2004, which rose to popularity in 2010. Although the TPM does not have a single leader, they are represented by national figures including Sarah Palin, Glenn Beck, Ron Paul, John Boehner and Michelle Bachmann. They are defined by a set of five extremely conservative core beliefs, which include "English as our core language is required," "reducing personal income tax is a must" and "traditional family values are encouraged."[46] Whether you believe the Tea Party's core values are essential for maintaining the constitution of the

United States, or you side with the fury of OWS, the way each group operates is essential to understanding generational narcissism.

Although the tea party was at its height of popularity in 2010, *unfavorable views* over the past three years and very *unfavorable* views have tripled. An October 2013 poll found that more than half of Americans reject the tea party and their values[47] (about the same favorability rating at OWS at its height in 2011), yet, during the same month, the group had the political power to shut down the American government for more than two weeks. Shortly after, TPM founder Rick Scarborough announced he would like to file a class action law suit against homosexuality; another action that may be favorable within a select group, but is met with disapproval by the United States as a whole. When it comes to understanding the rise in narcissism, this isn't an issue of left vs. right (do we even know that OWS is aligned with the left?), it is a battle between the approaches of Baby Boomers and Gen-Y. Whether or not OWS is justified in their movement, they operate with fingers pointed. Their politics are no more radical than that of the tea party, but their message, loud and clear is *this mess is not our fault and we aren't going to fix it.*

This is the New Normal

Now you know what keeps psychologists and sociologists up at night. Quite simply, the millennials are unequipped to take over the world they are inheriting. The thing is, even with hard evidence and years of research, Generation Y (whose non-rebellion seems to rebel against the values that defined Generation X) is happy with how they move through the world. Whether this is caused by inherent narcissism, or something else, they are optimistic that they have the world under control. In February 2013, blogger Matt Bors made waves when a series of editorial cartoons addressing the perception of millennials was posted on CNN.com. In the first cartoon, two young people are presented, one gazing into a cell phone and the other holding and armful of trophies. Throughout several cartoons, Bors confronts the core concerns that Generation X and the Baby Boomers have about Generation Y.[48] The theme throughout is externalization of blame (hello, narcissism). He blamed the stereotypes—from delaying adulthood, to not working on the mistakes and messes made by previous generations. If nothing else, Bors' take on the challenges faced by his generation is an important reminder that more than research and statistics are necessary to convince a generation who was taught that feeling is more important than thinking. Understanding the position of Generation Y, we must also ask ourselves "is it pathology if everyone is doing it?"

Chapter 4

KEEPING IN TOUCH OR LOSING TOUCH WITH REALITY?

"The production of too many useful things results in too many useless people."

– Karl Marx

"We must work passionately and indefatigably to bridge the gulf between our scientific progress and our moral progress. One of the great problems of mankind is that we suffer from a poverty of the spirit which stands in glaring contrast to our scientific and technological abundance. The richer we have become materially, the poorer we have become morally and spiritually."

– Martin Luther King Jr.

On August 8, 2013, Derek Medina shot and killed his wife in their Florida home. Moments later, his friends and family found out about it on Facebook. The 31-year-old father posted a photo of his wife's crumpled and bloodied body with the caption "Im going to prison or death sentence for killing my wife love you guys miss you guys takecare Facebook people you will see me in the news [sic]." The horrific image stayed online, and was shared thousands of times for about five hours before Facebook was notified and able to remove it.[49] Less than a month later, Ohio man Matthew Cordle filmed a video confessing to the hit-and-run killing of a 61-year-old veteran after a night of heavy drinking. The video went viral shortly after being posted on a popular video sharing website.[50] Around the country, dozens of high school and college students have been indicted on rape charges after posting pictures and bragging about the assaults online.

Why is this happening? What reason would a person have for sharing the shameful details of crimes on the Internet? Certainly there is nothing new about bragging after a heinous crime. More than a hundred years before social networking existed, Jack the Ripper wrote a series of taunting letters to the police and media. During the 1960s and 1970s, the Zodiac Killer sent two dozen letters to the police. This is pretty typical behavior for a narcissist, who believes he is above the law. To this day, neither Jack the Ripper nor the Zodiac Killer has been identified with any certainty. In these cases, both men successfully outwitted law enforcement. The only thing that has changed between now and then is that dangerous, sociopathic narcissists have more outlets for sharing their crimes. Technology makes bragging about crimes much easier than in the past. A drunken college student probably won't take the time to pen a letter to the police detailing a brutal sexual assault on a teen girl, but it only takes a few seconds to take a photo with a smart phone and share the heinous acts instantly.

It is impossible for me diagnose these braggart criminals with NPD, but I can point out that most operate with a high level of narcissist traits. Derek Medina—the man, who posted pictures of his dead wife—for example, was a self-proclaimed self-help writer, who professed to have saved marriages, made all of his dreams come true, and promised that the six books he wrote in six months will "change your world in seconds, days, months, years." It takes only a few minutes of browsing through his website, entitled "The Emotional Writer," to understand that there is something deeply wrong with his sense of self. In a writing style void of standard grammar and punctuation, he makes remarkable claims about his abilities, accomplishment and goals. Although his writings make no indication that he may be violent, his grandiosity and inflated self-image are apparent. It is safe to assert that any person who brags about a violent crime has a pathological level of arrogance consistent with narcissistic traits.

Social Networking for the Rest of Us

On a Saturday afternoon, I sit in a downtown Los Angeles bar working on my book. A group of Chicago hockey fans yell loudly and people all around have their cell phones out, as they take pictures of each other, and update their social networking sites with the score of the game and the name of the celebrity sitting in the corner. I take a break to check my Facebook page, after bragging that I am, in fact, writing a book in a bar during a hockey game, and a comedian I have admired for 20 years is sitting in the corner. Today, like on any given day, I am privy to the inconsequential details of my friend's lives. One friend lost her voice and needs vitamin C. Another is at the beach; and one needs advice on her yeast infection—*yikes*! Several people have posted pictures of what they ate for lunch, or simply posted their calorie count for the day. A dozen friends link news articles with their own political commentary and picture after picture of smiling babies and dancing toddlers fill my news feed. I could go on describing the inside jokes, personal rants, and delicate information, but there is no need. Sharing every detail with every person in one's life is the new normal.

If you ask your friends why they use social networking sites, like Facebook (I realize that by the time you read this, Facebook may be obsolete, so fill in the blank with whatever is popular), they will likely give you the most common reason given by anyone asked. "It helps me keep in touch with friends and family." Of course, this is true. Most people do in fact "friend" their parents, grandparents, cousins and a handful of childhood playmates. They share pictures of their children with friends who may never get a chance to see them in real life, and share pictures of their meals with people eating a less exciting meal. Social networking creates a universe centered on the individual. Until recently, there was no way for a narcissist to broadcast life details efficiently. Talking about one's self and devaluing others took effort. It would have taken hours to call everyone you know to tell them even your most important news. A 2013 study found that there is a distinction between the NPI scores of a social media user and the social media of choice. The study explained that Twitter is used as a microphone (to broadcast opinions and ideas), while Facebook is used as a mirror (to indulge vanity).[51] No matter the intent, Facebook and other social networking outlets offer unique opportunities to people with and without narcissistic tendencies that weren't available to previous generations. These opportunities directly coincide with traits of narcissism measured on the NPI.

Exhibitionism. is usually the first narcissistic behavior that comes to mind when considering the effects of social media. Exhibitionism is the trait that coincides with people sharing their every activity, mundane thoughts, and posting photos of food. Although much of this exhibitionism may seems harmless, people share more than boring details. A 2010 report found that 40% of social media users make comments and posts regarding alcohol use and even more post photos of themselves drinking. Half of users use profanity, a quarter post provocative or semi-nude photos, and many more post *sexy* photos showcasing cleavage or other sexualized body parts. Twenty percent of Facebook and Twitter users have made comments about their own sexual activities. Other common social networking faux pas include making racial slurs and complaining about employers. The study found that people who share potentially damaging information are proud of their over-sharing and feel that the exposure makes them look more attractive, cool, and popular. Even users who want to portray a clean, wholesome image are guilty of exhibitionism, as they post pictures and share life details intended to promote that persona.[52]

Vanity. For the somatic narcissist, whose self-image is dependent on sexuality, physical appearance, and material possessions, vanity is the most important tool in the social networking box. Social networking makes indulging vanity easier than ever before. For many, the goal of sharing a Facebook picture is to look *hot*. After a picture is posted, friends can comment on the picture, letting the user know how he or she looks. Because posting online is deliberate (as opposed to being seen at the grocery store or the gym, where the environment is out of control) each picture or witty statement is carefully crafted to project a specific image. Because time and effort is put into these projections, some type of response is expected from friends. Usually, the expected response is admiration, approval, or even envy. While everyone enjoys getting compliments or being recognized, vanity becomes unhealthy—even narcissistic—when approval is consistently needed to feel good. Some social media users post pictures of themselves—called *selfies*—several times a week or even per day. Common places for selfies are the gym (to let everyone know they work out), the car (probably because they checked themselves out in the rear view mirror), in bed (to show how good they look just waking up, or possibly to allude to sex), and even in the hospital (for sympathy).

Authority. In general, authority refers to a person's power and leadership skills. Oftentimes, this is healthy (for example, parents must have authority over their children and managers must have authority over their employees) but narcissistic authority occurs when an individual desires authority for the sake of power alone. Social media and blogging are both popular ways to maintain authority on a subject, and this behavior is more common with cerebral narcissists. In social media, this commonly comes from sharing authoritative information, such as an opinion on a political issue or important health information. These acts can be informative and they can also open dialogue, but they can also alienate people within a group, particularly when the information shared is controversial. My own experience and an informal survey found that politics and parenting issues are the most polarizing topics discussed on social media. A Pew research study found that nearly 20 percent of Facebook users block friends or even remove friends from their news feeds to avoid reading political posts.

Superiority. Any online activity that puts the user in a place of being *better* than anyone else is a display of superiority. Behavior consistent with superiority can be similar to establishing authority, especially in a cerebral narcissist who feels he or she is more intelligent than others. However, people can feel superior in many ways including the brand of phone they use, the parenting methods they use, the universities they attended, the clothing they wear, the religion they practice or the parties they attend. Several memes that are shared on Facebook, Instagram, and other sites make specific references to *stupid people*, assuming that the person sharing the meme is somehow superior. For example, one popular meme says. "I'm not saying let's go kill all the stupid people…I'm just saying let's remove all the warning labels and let the problem sort itself out."

Exploitativeness. in social networking comes in many shapes. In its least extreme type among average social networking users it usually comes in the form of *content farming*. This happens when a group or organization posts a provocative picture with instructions to "like" or "share" to support a vague cause such as stopping childhood cancer, ending animal cruelty, and often letting Jesus know you love him. This increases the views and shares that a page has, in turn increasing advertising revenue. These exploitative pictures are often pictures of sick kids or injured animals. The average user is not aware that any damage is being done and often feels guilty for *not* sharing. A more direct method of exploiting others is similar to the tactics used to establish superiority, but use the misfortunes of others. Common examples include sharing pictures of a person dressed terribly or doing something embarrassing. The people represented in the photos, of course are real people being exploited to entertain strangers. In one example, a Maryland Woman, Kelly Martin Broderick, posed for a picture holding a sign that said, "This is what a feminist looks like." The intended purpose, as part of a campaign sponsored by her University, was to present a vast array of women—and men—who are feminists. Broderick is overweight, and before long, her image was used as a widely circulated meme with the caption, "That's pretty much what I expected." The image also collected more than a thousand comments including: "This is also what a lifelong virgin looks like", and "Fat, old, angry and single. If they still have a sex drive they find another angry lesbian feminist and make each other and the people around them miserable." Broderick contacted Facebook, where the image was circulating, and was told that the photo did not break the site's privacy standards. In any case, she was exploited so that strangers could laugh at her weight and feminists in general. The most extreme form of social media exploitation is the heinous acts described in the beginning of this chapter, such as sharing violent acts against people. Thankfully, this is rare, but is becoming increasingly common.

A Shift in Cultural Norms

Pathology has been conceptualized in many ways, but should always be considered in the context of cultural norms. Twenty years ago, if you broadcast your opinions, what you are eating and where you are going as often as today's average Facebook user does, your friends and family would be very concerned and considerably annoyed. Because narcissistic behavior is embraced by so many healthy people, it is difficult to know if something is wrong or if times are just changing. Most aspects of our society change over time, and things that were once outrageous hardly garner any attention at all. Women freely vote, wear pants and use birth control with no resistance from culture at large. Biracial marriage, which was once illegal, is widely accepted and homosexuality is no longer a barrier to a satisfying life. Most Americans look back on a time when women, racial minorities and homosexuals were treated as second class citizens with shame and disgust. If we know now that our new attitudes are right, isn't it possible that other social changes are part of an evolving society? Remember American's reaction to Madonna's cone bra? Or the great "wardrobe malfunction" of 2004? That is nothing compared to an average night in the life of Miley Cyrus today.

Narcissism is more concerning than just a shift in cultural norms because it is harmful. People whose narcissism never reaches a diagnostic level can still destroy their own lives and the people they love with attention-seeking, egocentric behavior. Narcissism expert Jean Twenge has compared the increase of narcissism to the increase of obesity in the United States. No amount of normalizing can make it healthy. Even more alarming, social norms are changing at an unprecedented rate. Here are some ways that technology has allowed a shift in cultural norms:

A Shift From Anonymity to Self-Promotion

When the Internet first gained popularity in the early 1990s, anonymity was the appeal to those who were unhappy with their identities in the real world. Chat rooms, message boards and even dating sites were a place where a person could be anyone else. Horror stories abound about unsuspecting romantics who found the person they fell in love with over the Internet was not the age, sex, or weight they had expected. The anonymity of the Internet also created a fertile environment for cowards to harass and abuse. Cyberbullying has become so serious that legislature has been passed to prevent and prosecute offenders.

Megan Meier was 13 when she met her first boyfriend, Josh on Myspace in 2006. Megan, who had been overweight since early childhood, had struggled with ADD, depression and low self-esteem her entire life. Things got better for Megan around the time she started her relationship with Josh. She left her public school for a private Catholic school, joined the volleyball team, and ended a tumultuous friendship with a catty neighbor girl. Throughout their six week relationship, Josh became an instrumental part of Megan's life. Megan rushed to talk to him every day after school. Megan's mother Tina was aware of the relationship and watched closely to make sure that the 16-year-old boy never chatted with her daughter in a way that was sexually inappropriate. In fact, Tina was so careful to protect her daughter that only she had Megan's Myspace password. Megan needed permission and supervision to log in.

Six weeks into the relationship, Josh told Megan that he didn't want to be her friend anymore because he heard she was not very nice to her friends. Megan was confused as things became even worse. Before long, Josh and several of Megan's friends used the social networking site to post terrible things about Megan. They called her fat and a slut, and the messages circulated quickly. Josh sent Megan one more message, telling her that the world would be better without her. The same day, Megan hung herself in her bedroom closet while her parents made dinner. She died the next day, three days before her fourteenth birthday.

Megan's parents tried to contact Josh, but his Myspace profile was deleted shortly after Megan's death. Several weeks after Megan's death, a neighbor contacted Tina and her husband, Ron, urging them to meet her. They met at the school, with a grief counselor in attendance. At the meeting, Ron and Tina were told that Josh never existed. He was created by 47-year-old Lori Drew and her husband, the parents of the girl with whom Megan had ended a friendship with earlier in the year. Tina and Ron were shocked. They had been friends with the Drew family for years and Megan had vacationed with them. After Megan's death, Ron and Tina comforted them, attended their birthday parties and even stored a Foosball table for the Drew family. Tina, who was a real estate agent, had helped the Drew family purchase their home when they moved to the neighborhood.

After a long legal battle, the court found that Drew was guilty only of violating Myspace user policy, and misdemeanor charges were thrown out. In 2009, the Megan Meier Cyberbullying Prevention Act was introduced in Congress. Clearly, covert Internet behavior is a problem recognized by the entire country and our government. So, how did it happen, that overt, self-promoting behaviors have become even more prevalent? There is no doubt that something was seriously wrong with Lori Drew. Most people can agree that is it abnormal for an adult woman to use her time and energy to bully an emotionally struggling child. Somehow, these same people are missing the unhealthy proportion of time and energy that young people are putting into exhibitionism.

A Shift from Introversion to Extroversion

This change could be in part due to a shift from introversion to extroversion. Consider the popular NBC television program *To Catch a Predator*. The hidden-camera reality show sets up stings across the country. Unsuspecting men think they are entering homes to meet children for sexual encounters. Instead, they are arrested after an awkward interview with host Chris Hansen. All of the men arrested during these stings have engaged in sexually explicit conversations online and made their intentions clear. Many of their online conversations are broadcast so that we can fully understand what the men expected when they walked into the house. Still, it is painfully clear that many of these men have weak social skills. There is no excuse for abusing a child, but you don't have to stretch your imagination too far to see that many of these men are socially inadequate and likely rejected in healthy adult interactions. These social introverts gain power through asserting themselves covertly online.

A Shift in Defining Relationships

Maintaining shallow relationships is a common narcissistic trait. Before social networking, such relationships, in healthy individuals, often fell by the wayside. Social networking has allowed us to "keep in touch" on a superficial level. One study found that Facebook users who have more than 354 friends are less satisfied with their lives than people whose online friendships more closely reflect real-life friendships.[53] A sociological phenomenon explains that when we see acquaintances in real life outside of context, we feel closer to them. A friend of mine went on a trip to Paris, France. While sitting at an outdoor café, she saw a woman who worked in another office in her building. They weren't friends, they had barely spoken more than a few words in the public restroom or while waiting for the elevator. They knew no details of each other's personal lives, but in Paris, thousands of miles from home, they embraced like old friends, and made plans to visit a museum together. Social networking mimics this once-rare social interaction every day. Suddenly, by way of seeing familiar faces out of context, we feel compelled to take an active part in the online lives of people we barely know, therefore establishing and maintaining shallow relationships. Social media users with higher levels of narcissism tend to pay close attention to the number of online "friends" they have, and are even willing to friend strangers. This is usually more about having an audience than interpersonal connections.

Intimate relationships are also affected by social media habits. In a world where life is defined by social media presence, the way a relationship *looks* online is very important—for better or worse. Susanne was married for nine years when she found out her husband had a 4-year-old son with another woman. He had been hiding money and lying, yet they agreed to stay together for their two children. Last week was their anniversary, and Susanne posted, "Happy 12th anniversary to the best husband and father in the world! We've had our ups and downs through the years, but I know we will always love each other. Thank you for everything you do for our family, babe!" Bad husbands in real life are gods among men online. This is especially apparent on Father's Day when transgressions are forgotten in favor of a happy post. Denial is a narcissistic trait, but so is a desire to inflate associates. Just like narcissists go to the *best* schools and have the *best* doctors, they have the best friends and romantic partners. There are other ways that social media users promote their *perfect* relationships, too. *Cosmopolitan* magazine pointed out that hashtags are often used to brag. The magazine said that the most common relationship hashtags used are #bestwife, #luckygirl, #lovemyhubby, #arentwecute and #sorrrynotsorry, the final being used to dismiss any possible accusations of narcissistic behavior. Using such hashtags is often a desperate attempt to *prove* happiness, which could really be a sign of dissatisfaction. Gushing is a similar problem. There's nothing wrong with projecting a happy life and great marriage, but really there is nothing novel about loving a spouse, that is what marriage is all about. I also find it really interesting when couples engage in a public discussion via social media. Wall posts such as *Can you pick up milk?... What should we get for dinner tonight?* And even *"I love you's"* are odd, because couples can talk face-to-face, send text messages, call, or even send private messages online. The only reason to do this online is to make sure others see...and react.

Men tend to do things differently. Highly narcissistic men may forget their romantic partners altogether. Lily and her boyfriend Tom were living together for a few months when Lily became concerned about Tom's social media use. Lily had no social media accounts, but Tom had several and was glued to his phone most of the day. She found that even though they seemed to get along fine, there was no mention of her existence on Facebook, Instagram, or Twitter. She didn't want to overreact, by being unable to separate real life from virtual life, but Tom had several female "friends" (naked, by the way, and whom she had never met or heard of). Eventually their relationship ended because Tom was unable to let go of those online connections and his online persona.

A Shift in Seeking Social Support

In 2008, Kenneth was enjoying a lucrative career, and living in a seventeenth century fisherman's cottage off the coast of France with his wife. Kenneth was in a terrible accident while driving to work, and was left with a broken back, chronic seizures and unbearable pain. "I fell into a deep, dark depression," Kenneth explained. "Being in constant pain all the while, not getting out of the house, laid up and useless. My new wife left me, and I can't really blame her, I was no fun anymore. I isolated myself, cooped up in my cottage, trying to mend. After one year of agony, I had decided enough was enough, studied the art of noose-making on the Internet, and hung myself with some rope that was lying around our little cottage. I let myself down. I thought of my friends and family that I was letting down, upsetting, and somehow, and I do not know to this day how I did it, for I made that noose well, I freed myself. I didn't want to think of an outpouring of grief on my Facebook. I had a plan, and I didn't want this very private moment to be a conversation topic."

Kenneth made the decision to continue his life, but he was still miserable and lonely. Finally, he turned to Facebook for social support. Through social networking, he made friends with a woman who came into his home and taught him about emotionally focused therapy, a short-term method of managing emotional responses. "She sat patiently with me for hours, teaching me how to climb out of my hole. If it weren't for Facebook, and a seemingly random friendship, I wouldn't be here." Kenneth's friendship and his improved emotional state led to new opportunities for online friendships. "Unexpectedly, a group of people, friends of this angel, befriended me, first online and then off. All with a common trait of humanity and love. Hippies, I used to call them, in a somewhat derogatory way. They shared meditations and motivational posts on my Facebook page. They shared a metaphorical snorkel to keep me breathing, even though I was well underwater at the time. I came to rely on their posts and messages of support and love on Facebook, and I opened my eyes to the spirit. For the first time in my life, they taught me how to listen to my inner self, to thank The Universe for small progress." Before long, Kenneth was strong enough to begin physical therapy. His physical therapist rented him her home with a stair lift. "Before long, I could make it to the local pub, where I met some of these wonderful Facebook friends for the first time. Friends not yet met, friends who probably still don't know to this day that they saved me."

Today, Kenneth's life is much different. He moved to the United States, and has essentially started over, with a new home, career, and many new friends. Still, he attributes his happiness and new life to the support he received online. "When you are housebound and lonely and hurting, it seems odd to say, in retrospect, that Facebook saved me. In reality, it was those friends found on there, those who scraped me up when I needed it most, their little hippy optimistic posts really made a difference, and I will forever remember and love them. It seems absurd to admit, that this Facebook channel of humanity, of connectedness, of common consciousness, that outpouring of love and compassion from friends not yet met, saved my life, and I endeavor to pour love and hope back into it. You never know when a simple post can save somebody. Even the post of a kitten can make a person's day."

Online support is also readily available for people dealing with chronic illness. When Regina was diagnosed with cancer at age 31, she went straight to social networking. She announced her terrifying diagnosis, and was immediately met with overwhelming social support. Her close friends and family were there for her, and so were more distant friends, and acquaintances. Throughout her year-long ordeal, she posted pictures and updates, letting everyone share in the pain, fear and hope she experienced every day of her illness. Using Internet outlets for social support during a personal crisis is becoming increasingly popular. And if there's a time in one's life when it's OK—maybe necessary to reach out, and in a sense say *look at me!* A University of Washington study reported, "Social support is a critical, yet underutilized resource when undergoing cancer care. Underutilization occurs in two conditions: (a) when patients fail to seek out information, material assistance, and emotional support from family and friends or (b) when family and friends fail to meet the individualized needs and preferences of patients. Social networks are most effective when kept up to date on the Patient's status, yet updating everyone takes effort that patients cannot always put in." Social networking seems to solve *all* of those problems and more. People suffering from serious illness can seek out information and support and with minimal effort, update everyone they know on how they are what they need. Problem solved.

I can't argue that increased support to those in need is a bad thing. Obviously, the social support garnered from social networking helped Kenneth and Regina, and it has helped others, too. Learning the experiences of others is another valuable tool in feeling hopeful when facing a daunting diagnosis. Stories of hope from strangers can be found all over the Internet, and most importantly, people facing tragedy feel less alone when they meet someone like them. Good things are happening. Still, it presents another shift in cultural norms. Whether it is good or bad, the way that our culture once approached a part of life and death has changed considerably (If you don't believe me, ask your grandfather how many people knew the details of his prostate surgery), and this is mostly related to changes in privacy concerns. More than about sharing private information, social networking has normalized sharing the nitty-gritty details of life. One example is the work of photographer Angelo Merendino; who documented his wife' battle with breast cancer. Since Jennifer Merendino passed in 2011, her husband has written a book, presented a gallery exhibition of his photos, and established a non-profit that provides financial assistance to women living with breast cancer. On his website, Merendino says:

> *Jen was in chronic pain from the side effects of nearly 4 years of treatment and medications. At 39 Jen began to use a walker and was exhausted from being constantly aware of every bump and bruise. Hospital stays of 10-plus days were not uncommon. Frequent doctor visits led to battles with insurance companies. Fear, anxiety and worries were constant. Sadly, most people do not want to hear these realities and at certain points we felt our support fading away. Other cancer survivors share this loss. People assume that treatment makes you better, that things become OK, that life goes back to "normal." However, there is no normal in cancer-land. Cancer survivors have to define a new sense of normal, often*

daily. And how can others understand what we had to live with everyday? My photographs show this daily life. They humanize the face of cancer, on the face of my wife. They show the challenge, difficulty, fear, sadness and loneliness that we faced, that Jennifer faced, as she battled this disease. Most important of all, they show our Love. These photographs do not define us, but they are us [sic].

There is nothing remotely wrong or unhealthy about Merendino's sentiments, and his works seems to be helping people in tremendous ways. What caught my attention however, was the interest in documenting an extremely private process. Because at one time, not very long ago, exhibiting photographs of a dying person was unheard of, and may have been regarded as tasteless, it is important to recognize this as a change in cultural norms, *even if we can agree the outcome is beneficial.*

A Shift in Defining Self

When maintaining an online profile of any kind—it is natural to want to use a good picture. This was true, before the Internet, when, as long as photography has existed (and probably also occurred when paintings were used to capture a person's likeness) people have rejected bad pictures. You know—the ones with closed eyes, open mouth or bad side. Bad pictures used to be part of life, and sometimes after years have passed, it *is* possible to like even the bad pictures because of the fun or special times they represented. Digital photography has been wonderful for weeding out bad pictures and keeping good pictures, but spending a significant amount of time working on the perfect "selfie" or *playing model* is a concern.

Aside from how we look, online sharing makes us feel important even when what we say isn't particularly important or interesting. For many people, a sense of self is strongly connected to online sharing and more importantly, the way others respond. Social networking involves a surplus of narcissistic activities, but they almost always involve interactions with others. One person posts something, and others respond. Blogging, on the other hand, is *all about the writer.* Just as social networking is healthy in some contexts, blogging can make a lot of sense. It provides a forum for expertise in an area, and is an effective way for a person going through a unique experience to share. For example, when a friend was adopting a child from Russia, she kept a blog so her friends and family could be kept up to date and share in the family's struggles. More often, however, blogging is a place where narcissistic traits come to light. Authority, self-sufficiency, superiority, and exhibitionism can all be indulged with a blog.

Bloggers have realized that bragging isn't always well-received, as not everyone likes to read about how perfect ordinary people are. Recently, it has become fashionable for bloggers to write about things that are hard for them, or tough stages in their lives. The purpose is to show how down-to-earth and relatable they are so others will respect their ideas and perceived authority. In a recent example, "mommy blogger" Alison Slater Tate wrote an article for *Brain Child* titled, "When My Tween Son Doesn't Love me." Her story starts with dropping her son off at school. When she tells him she loves him, he responds, "I don't love you" and rudely slams the door.[54] Instead of explaining ways that a parent can talk to children about disrespectful behavior Slater Tate normalizes back-talk and oppositional defiance as though it is a normal stage of development. In case a reader wonders if she has thought about discipline and enforcing respect, she explains that their good moments come when she surprises him with a book or allows him to stay up late in her bed. What I found most interesting was the online comments. Instead of berating her for permissive parenting, which so often happens online, readers praised her. All struggling parents deserve support, but broadcasting parenting deficiencies and other personal problems once referred to as "airing dirty laundry" is now "being real."

A recent British study found that people with narcissistic tendencies overwhelmingly see themselves as creative and engage in creative activities, such as art and writing, and dancing. There is no evidence that narcissistic people are in fact more creative (although they are likely to be more confident and persuasive) but the Internet provides a medium for this perceived creativity. In addition to blogs, people who enjoy all types of creativity can share on websites like Pinterest, an "online pinboard to collect and share what inspires you."

A Shift in Social Comparisons

Social comparisons are not new. Since the beginning of time, people have been aware of what other have and do. Because friends can use social networking to update life's ups and downs, we use social comparisons to evaluate our own lives and happiness more than ever. A friend bought a new house in a great neighborhood, I'm jealous. A friend's teenage son ran away *again*, I'm relieved it's not *my* kid. It's normal to use the experiences of others as a baseline for our own. Unfortunately, because people tend to inflate what they share, we are often left with a very skewed window to reality. One study found that people who use Facebook several times a day are less happy than those who use it moderately or infrequently.[55] A German study found that 1 in 3 people feel a sense of sadness and dissatisfaction with their lives after browsing Facebook. People who read without posting are affected more. Teenagers are especially susceptible to this because their level of development, combined with limited life experience makes it more difficult to understand the difference between real life and the pieces of life represented online. The research found, however, that adults in their 30s were most jealous over pictures and posts depicting a happy family. Women were more jealous than men over physical attractiveness. Men became more jealous over the accomplishments of their friends.

A Shift from Stalking to Cyber Stalking

Before my sister goes on a date with a new man, I Google him. In graduate school, a clinical practice professor presented the struggle of whether or not to search for a client online as an ethical dilemma.

I often spend a few minutes trying to find out what I can about my kids' teachers. When a friend was having trouble with her ex-husband, she "unfriended" any mutual friends they shared. Another friend spent hours each week looking for *dirt* on her husband's ex-girlfriend. Searching for a friend, acquaintance, childhood friend or former lover online is a common practice in a day and age when technology is available at all times. Most of the time, this behavior is not serious or threatening, and violent acts rarely result.

Officially called *obsessive relational intrusion,* it is commonly known as *cyber stalking.* A 2011 study identified 12 potentially dangerous behaviors common in real-world stalking relationships, and found that each had an equivalent in the cyber world. For example, a traditional stalker may follow his victim to and from work, school, and other activities. A tech-savvy stalker, on the other hand can follow her victim's "check-ins" and gain insight about his activities. A traditional stalker may have tried to initiate contact with her victim's friends and relatives by inviting them to events, or showing up at their jobs. A Facebook stalker, on the other hand can *friend* the friends and relatives of the victim, or contact them online. When it comes to stalkers, the thoughts, feelings, goals and tactics have not changed. However, technology has made it much easier to find and maintain victims.[56] As discussed in previous chapters, narcissists, even those diagnosed with NPD are not necessarily anti-social. However, characteristics of NPD, such as an inability to understand the views of others, lack of empathy, boundary issues and a sense of entitlement can really make an ordinary narcissist cross-over the anti-social line more easily than healthy people.

A Shift in Privacy Expectations

Rachel and Stephen were enjoying a dream honeymoon. Their friends followed their adventures, as the couple updated their joint Facebook page. "At the Eiffel Tower" captioned a picture of the newlyweds kissing high above Paris. "Swimming in the French Riviera" was an update that popped up two days later. Later in the week "at the airport, time to get back to the real world" captioned a photo of Stephen dragging heavy suitcases through the airport. And finally, "OMG we've been robbed! Our wedding presents R gone." with a picture of their home, clearly ransacked. As people share more, and trust more on weak online privacy settings, such burglaries are becoming more common. In 2010, a burglary ring in New Hampshire stole more than $200,000 worth of property, all from vacationing families. In 2012, a similar operation in the Portland, Oregon area stole nearly as much, including four cars. The trend has also caught on in U.K. One Nashville couple who boasted about expensive possessions was burglarized while they were gone only a few hours at a concert. The police never identified the person or people responsible for breaking into Rachel and Stephen's home, and stealing thousands of dollars' worth of house wares, jewelry and video game systems. They both deny that any of their Facebook friends could have done something so terrible. While people may trust their friends, the truth is that if a friend comments on or "likes" a status, their friends can see the original post. This means that personal information is potentially available to thousands of strangers.

A sharp juxtaposition exists between online privacy concerns and online self-promotion. The same population who shares photos, their exact locations, and personal phone numbers online simultaneously demands more privacy. Half of young adults under 30 resent surrendering personal privacy to government programs (namely, the National Security Agency, or NSA) that follow Internet activity to combat terrorism. In the same survey, 91% of children ages 12-17 reported posting pictures online. An overwhelming majority posted the name of their school, the city they live in, and their email addresses. When it comes to teens and online privacy, however, they are much less concerned with what strangers, advertisers or the NSA see and more worried about how people they know (parents, teachers, adults from the community) will react to their online behavior.[57] Instead of working to shape the way young people view online privacy and protect themselves, we are sweeping in like helicopter parents to protect them. In 2013, California Governor Jerry Brown signed a bill to increase privacy for minors. The bill required that websites, mobile phone apps and other online services allow users an option to remove or delete information they posted as minors. In his statement, Senate President pro tem Darrel Steinberg said, "This is a groundbreaking protection for our kids who often act impetuously with postings of ill-advised pictures or messages before they think through the consequences. They deserve the right to remove this material that could haunt them for years to come."[58]

Those who Can't, Comment

Since 1872, *Popular Science* magazine has been the leading magazine in its genre. For over a century, it has successfully circulated scientific information in a way accessible to the average person. After *Popular Science* launched online content, it began to face a problem met by every online media outlet: comments. Online readers can comment on news stories, blog entries, and opinion pieces across the web. Some of the comments are insightful, and provide an alternate perspective, sparking lively and thoughtful conversation. Other times, online comments are inflammatory, or uninformed. The forum is also sometimes used for advertising and spam, unrelated to the content of the website. After 141 years in print and over a decade online, *Popular Science* made the decision to disable online comments. On their website, they addressed this issue with the following statement:

> Even a fractious minority wields enough power to skew a reader's perception of a story, recent research suggests. In one study led by University of Wisconsin-Madison professor Dominique Brossard, 1,183 Americans read a fake blog post on nanotechnology and revealed in survey questions how they felt about the subject (are they wary of the benefits or supportive?). Then, through a randomly assigned condition, they read either epithet- and insult-laden

comments ("If you don't see the benefits of using nanotechnology in these kinds of products, you're an idiot") or civil comments.

The results, as Brossard and coauthor Dietram A. Scheufele wrote in a *New York Times* op-ed:

> *Uncivil comments not only polarized readers, but they often changed a participant's interpretation of the news story itself. In the civil group, those who initially did or did not support the technology — whom we identified with preliminary survey questions—continued to feel the same way after reading the comments. Those exposed to rude comments, however, ended up with a much more polarized understanding of the risks connected with the technology. Simply including an ad hominem attack in a reader comment was enough to make study participants think the downside of the reported technology was greater than they'd previously thought.*[59]

The lesson? The opinions, even the nasty ones, of laypeople tend to influence opinion as much as fact based on years of expertise, research and work. In this case, the narcissistic behavior is not coming from the know-it-all experts, but from the average Joe who thinks his opinion is more important—or more correct—than that of the professionals. I know what you're thinking. *Everyone's opinion is important!* That is somewhat true, and also somewhat the aftermath of the self-esteem indoctrination discussed in Chapter 3. Everyone *is* entitled to his or her opinion. One example of a time when a person feels the need to express an uneducated opinion is in any matter relating to religion. Articles about hot-button topics such as marriage equality and abortion, for example, elicit angry, off-topic comments usually pointing to religious beliefs. I understand that people feel it is their *duty* to defend their religious beliefs. Ignoring an opportunity to stand up for beliefs is, by some people, considered cowardly, or as a spiritual failure. However, engaging in a spiteful argument with a stranger does little to boost the faith of others. Nobody will convert religions or switch political parties based on a nasty online comment. As for everyone else, why should their opinion matter? In most cases, provocative comments are made by rabble-rousers who get their kicks from upsetting others and inciting debate. These types of comments get more attention than kind or supportive comments, and tend to result in others holding faster to their original beliefs.

Mother Jones magazine, a liberal outlet that in their own words is "a nonprofit news organization that specializes in investigative, political, and social justice reporting"[60] has dealt with their share of trolls. *Mother Jones'* position is highly polarized, resulting in strong feelings from opposition. The magazine's climate change editors became curious about a specific heckler, who in one month, tweeted about *Mother Jones* 126 times, more than their top 9 followers combined. This *troll* turned out to be Hoyt Connell, a middle-aged insurance executive who wears argyle sweaters and likes cats. Hoyt Connell is a *normal* guy. *Mother Jones* reporters, James West and Tim McDonald took the opportunity to interview Connell in his home, and presented the 3-part interview series on their website. Connell is no blubbering idiot, as one may expect an Internet troll to be. He is well-dressed, well-groomed, and although his speech is a bit aggressive at times, he is respectful and well-spoken throughout the interview. He is rather likeable, and the journalists compared him to an uncle who wants to debate over Thanksgiving dinner. During the interview, Connell shared interesting information. For example, his penchant for Internet research began after he was diagnosed with prostate cancer, which he victoriously survived. Unfortunately, most of his arguments were trite, and based on limited knowledge, which is apparent no matter where you stand on the political issues. For example, he says of global warming, "It is a theory that has been usurped by politics." He accuses Congressman Henry Waxman (who he admits to distrusting because he is a Democrat) of not doing his "homework" but offers no real information or formed counter-argument. In the final portion of the recorded interview Connell discusses the issue with Yale University Nuclear Physicist, Rosi Reed. Reed, who has a Ph.D., is equipped to discuss the distinction between journalism and science (the average person learns about most scientific topics, including global warming, from the media. Typically, only scholars access peer-reviewed journals where scientific studies are published. Therefore, homegrown "experts" whose knowledge comes from Internet "research" usually come from journalists, who are not necessarily experts themselves in the topics they cover.), and tries to address Connell's concerns. For example, Reed explains a bit about the scientific process, which is often unknown by, or ignored by the public. She believes that the ease of accessing the Internet has made average people feel that they know as much as experts who have studied their respective field for years. She wishes that people would ask questions about ideas they don't understand instead of calling names or vehemently denying data obtained through legitimate research. Video editing may be to blame, but during the interaction, Connell was unable to offer anything concrete, and once again, blamed politics and money for propagating a scientific issue.[61]

Of course, not all online comments are bad. People of all backgrounds are experts of their own lives and own experiences. Your opinion on a book, a vacuum cleaner, or a resort in Mexico could be a valuable tool to help a stranger make a good decision or avoid a bad experience. Online commenting and similar behaviors only become narcissistic when the commenter believes his or her opinions are more valuable than that of others, and that his or her knowledge surpasses the knowledge, or is somehow more complete than that of true experts.

Checking in or Checked out?

Checking in online is an indirect (dare I say passive-aggressive?) way to share information, and usually is meant for bragging or sharing bad news. In Chapter 3, we discussed fame being perceived as happiness for an increasing number of Americans. Checking-in at a restaurant, club, sporting event, airport, or resort lets friends know how exclusive, cool, or rich you are and lets everyone know you are having fun. If you check-in at the hospital or funeral home, no explanation is needed. Your friends will all ask you what is wrong, and offer thoughts and prayers. I don't know very many people who check in at embarrassing locations, such as the local jail, or STD clinic, but I'm sure it has happened. As reality and virtual reality become more enmeshed, the social media message is that if you didn't check in, it didn't happen. Telling our personal story and *checking in* is certainly part of the human experience. When I was a child, my grandparents showed me pictures and videos of their road trips. When American astronauts were the first to land on the moon, the American flag was firmly planted into the soil. Cavemen made pictures on walls. Just like *some* narcissism is healthy, some checking-in is healthy. Modern technology has allowed ordinary people to reach an unhealthy level of self-promotion.

Companies have cashed in on our desire for self-promotion. Foursquare, one of the many companies that facilitates social media check-ins, crowns a *lucky* user "mayor" of a location if he or she is the most frequent patron of that location. That's right—if you go to the corner bar more than any other person for two months; you are mayor of that bar! Companies, including Starbucks, city transit systems, and television networks offer coupons and special deals to the mayor and other frequent users. Sure, these programs offer great deals to people who want them, which should be a win-win in advertising. The problem is that our penchant for self-promotions and self-sharing is being used as free advertising.

Aside from the concerns related to privacy, self-promotion, and operating as living advertisements, there is valid concern that focusing on a check-in takes away from a real experience. Can a person be truly *in the moment* when posting online, thinking about posting online, and checking for responses? Comedian Louis C.K. discussed this problem as a guest on *Late Night With Conan O'Brien*:

You need to build an ability to just be yourself and not be doing something. That's what the phones are taking away, is the ability to just sit there. That's being a person. Because underneath everything in your life there is that thing, that empty—forever empty. That knowledge that it's all for nothing and that you're alone. It's down there. And sometimes when things clear away, you're not watching anything, you're in your car, and you start going, 'oh no, here it comes. That I'm alone.' It's starts to visit on you [*sic*]. Just this sadness. Life is tremendously sad, just by being in it. That's why we text and drive. I look around, pretty much 100 percent of the people driving are texting. And they're killing, everybody's murdering each other with their cars. But people are willing to risk taking a life and ruining their own because they don't want to be alone for a second because it's so hard.

Louis is right. Although some people criticized his point of view (one blogger called it crap, plenty of others used more colorful language) interestingly, a lot of people agreed with him, and the video of his appearance went viral. His explanation (sometimes called a rant) was described as "brilliant" and "masterful." An op-ed in the *Los Angeles Times* called him a "holy man." Somehow, Louis was able to explain something that experts know and the general public ignores in a way that made sense and touched nerves. After the initial days of reaction, life turned back to normal in cyberspace. Faces were buried in smart phones, selfies resumed. We all went back to *normal.* In a day and age where everyone can engage in behavior that was once only narcissistic, we must ask if we are keeping touch or losing touch with reality.

Chapter 5

THE REALITY TV MENTALITY

"I had a boyfriend who told me I'd never succeed, never be nominated for a Grammy, never have a hit song, and that he hoped I'd fail. I said to him, 'Someday, when we're not together, you won't be able to order a cup of coffee at the fucking deli without hearing or seeing me."

– Lady Gaga

I'm Nobody! Who are you?
Are you – Nobody – too?
Then there's a pair of us?
Don't tell! they'd advertise – you know!

How dreary – to be – Somebody!
How public – like a Frog –
To tell one's name – the livelong June –
To an admiring Bog!

– Emily Dickinson

You don't have to have magic unicorn powers. You work at it, and you get better. It's like anything: You sit there and do it every day, and eventually you get good at it.

—Kathleen Hanna

Fame has long been linked to narcissism, and it is no wonder that people who thrive in the spotlight also have higher levels of narcissistic traits, such as confidence, extroversion, likability, vanity, a desire to be liked and a sense of being different. This makes sense, considering famous people need a *special something* to combat stage fright and be comfortable in the public eye. Celebrities in all areas of the entertainment industry tend to have higher scores on the NPI than average adults.[62] The public has also been long interested in celebrities. For most of Hollywood history, however, what we know of stars has come from magazine articles and exclusive interviews. The information shared has historically been protected by publicists, so as to maintain some sense of privacy for the rich and famous. In the past decade, however, changes in entertainment have led to changes in fame and the way celebrity has been viewed. Reality TV, in particular, gives fame to people whose lack of talent would have ruled out a career in entertainment only a few years ago.

Reality TV viewers are privy to the inconsequential details of celebrity lives, such as shopping, eating, working out, and arguing. Every reality television personality shares an important narcissistic trait—they believe that the public *cares* about the mundane details of their lives. A study of NPI scores among celebrities found that reality stars have the highest level of narcissistic traits in their personalities, followed by actors and actresses, comedians, and lastly, musicians.[62] This is interesting, because in general, reality stars tend to have the lowest skill set among celebrities (remember, these people get famous for being outrageous, rich, sleeping with certain other famous people, or simply getting pregnant) and musicians, who have the lowest level of narcissism, tend to have the highest skill set. The study that examined these traits found that the length of a time an individual had enjoyed celebrity status (more specifically, been paid for what they do) had no influence on narcissistic traits, indicating that narcissistic traits were likely present before celebrity status was obtained. Our celebrity-obsessed society rewards the narcissistic tendencies of the famous, by treating them as special. Everyone has heard a story of a celebrity getting away with a crime (or literally getting away with murder) and wondered how it was possible.

Of course, it makes sense that reality television is made up of narcissistic personalities. First, a person must have a desire to appear on television, even when there is a risk of looking foolish; and stay on television, after looking foolish has become a reality. Second, producers choose people who are likeable, and we know that narcissists are almost always initially charming. Finally, television producers desire participants who can create drama, and in the case of competition shows, behave competitively. Happy, easy-going people make for boring television.

Pulling reality television apart is a book in its own. Reality television is a hub for racial and gender stereotypes, as well as classism, but it also says quite a bit about narcissism today. For one, reality television normalizes narcissistic behavior by perpetuating the narcissistic belief that one is special, entitled, and deserving of fame, without the contingency of talent or hard work. A 2013 study found that people who watch voyeuristic and competition reality programs have higher levels of narcissistic traits than people who watch educational reality television or no reality programming at all. The sitcoms that previous generations grew up watching have been criticized for being unrealistic or promoting gender stereotypes. We've all had a laugh about June Cleaver cleaning the house in heels and a pearl necklace, wondered who would buy that a married couple sleeps in separate beds, or cringed at the thought of Ricky spanking Lucy for buying an expensive hat. Believe me—I know that traditional programming had its weaknesses. Still, television shows, especially those aimed at children and teens, attempted to promote values and portray characters as growing, developing people *trying* to do the right thing. I know that the shows I enjoyed as a kid during the 1980s were filled with coming-of-age struggles that usually ended with lessons learned. Reality television, on the other hand, is full of back-stabbing at worst, and crying over spilt milk, at best.

Another concern is that this commercial reality sends a misleading message that superficial love, material objects (sometimes based on fake wealth) and beauty (more often based on fake body parts) are somehow related to a sense of self, or sense of reality. Even competition shows that focus on talent and ability feature personalities who care about their own success and self-interest more than the wellbeing of others. Of equal concern is the prevalence of fame for celebrity's sake. Even though our obsession with celebrity has existed for years, at one point, we respected and admired the art that typically preceded celebrity status, and at one time, celebrities also honored that art.

Consider the life and death of Kurt Cobain, the front man for 90's grunge rock band, Nirvana. Cobain was a dedicated musician and fame just sort of happened (without the help of YouTube or a competition reality show). Even after the band's album sold 10 million copies across the globe, Cobain wore torn jeans and flannel shirts, and purportedly purchased at thrift shops. Nearly twenty years after his death, his signature sneakers can be purchased for about $25 at any Target store. All three members of the band were known to eat lunch at *7-11*, and Cobain often complained of not being able to get his favorite meal, *Kraft* macaroni and cheese, when traveling. At the time of his death in 1994, his only car was a 1978 *Volvo*, although he took cabs during his last days because he had a flat tire; and he lived in an ordinary home in rural Washington. If it weren't for a $500 a day heroin habit, one might think Cobain was cheap. The truth was, he hated fame as much as he loved music, and the pressure of being famous was too much for him. In his suicide note, he wrote:

> When we're back stage and the lights go out and the manic roar of the crowds begin, it doesn't affect me the way in which it did for Freddie Mercury, who seemed to love, relish in the love and adoration from the crowd which is something I totally admire and envy. The fact is, I can't fool you, any one of you. It simply isn't fair to you or me. The worst crime I can

think of would be to rip people off by faking it and pretending as if I'm having 100% fun. Sometimes I feel as if I should have a punch-in time clock before I walk out on stage. I've tried everything within my power to appreciate it (and I do, God, believe me I do, but it's not enough). I appreciate the fact that I and we have affected and entertained a lot of people. I must be one of those narcissists who only appreciate things when they're gone.

How interesting, that this man, tortured by his fame, unable to ever get comfortable with being rich and famous could believe that he might be a narcissist. The entire point of voyeuristic reality programs is to make viewer believe that *there is no punch-in time clock* for the famous- the cameras are following them all day long. I recently watched a reality television program in which a woman, while planning her wedding made several phone calls to vendors, explaining that she was planning a wedding for a celebrity. When asked which celebrity, she replied that she could not divulge that information. The irony, of course, is that her ridiculous narcissism is hilarious to watch, and garners ratings like nothing else, making her something of a celebrity.

Fake it Until You Make it (Or Pay for it)

If you can't make it as a celebrity, you can pay to be treated like a celebrity. Rebecca Black was only fourteen years old when she became an overnight Internet sensation. Unfortunately for her, her notoriety came after being mocked by comedians on television and the web. The music video for her song "Friday" went viral, but for its absolutely terrible lyrics and vocal performance. Despite her song being dubbed "the worst song of the year" and earning nearly four million "dislikes" on YouTube within two months of going viral, Rebecca did in fact become famous. She made appearances on late night television shows, morning talk shows, and was featured in a Katy Perry music video. Her song was even covered on an episode of *Glee*. Her career started with a $4,000 check her mother wrote to Ark Music Factory, a company that writes pop songs and creates professional music videos for a hefty fee. Instead of Black's embarrassment deterring other fame-hungry kids, her fame made Ark more popular than ever. They have continued to turn out music videos, filled with awkward lyrics, bad auto-tuned music, over-sexualized children and routine rap interludes. One video featured a tween girl singing about her struggle to get away from the paparazzi, and her video depicts her ducking away from screaming fans—pretty ironic considering she is paying big bucks to pretend that anybody would recognize her. In October 2013, Ark released a video with a teen hungry for more than just cheap fame. The video for twelve-year-old Alison's Gold's song "Chinese Food" starts with her singing about food and ends with her frolicking with a panda. Don't forget the racism in-between as several Asian stereotypes (including girls dressed in geisha regalia, which is Japanese, not Chinese) are presented. These videos, like countless other paid-to-feel-famous options available today, are not a celebration of hard work or talent, but a celebration of narcissistic self. In addition to these frightening values, many parents forget that child stars (and celebrities in general) have a long-standing reputation for depression, substance abuse, legal troubles and suicide. If celebrity status can't cure the ailments of the highly talented, it surely won't solve the problems of ordinary folks.

Chapter 6

MONEY, MONEY, MONEY

"Whoever said money can't buy happiness was obviously a rich person lying to a group of poor people."

—Daniel Kibblesmith and Sam Weiner, *How to Win at Everything*

"This planet has - or rather had - a problem, which was this: most of the people living on it were unhappy for pretty much of the time. Many solutions were suggested for this problem, but most of these were largely concerned with the movement of small green pieces of paper, which was odd because on the whole it wasn't the small green pieces of paper that were unhappy."

– Douglas Adams, *The Hitchhiker's Guide to the Galaxy*

"Too many people spend money they earned ...to buy things they don't want. . . to impress people that they don't like."

– Will Rogers

More than any other source, the media is responsible for telling us what we need and when we need it. Our societal narcissism benefits a wide range of industries- from auto makers to clothing designers. In Chapter three, we discussed many of the social problems plaguing

China today. Although many Chinese citizens and outside sociologists understand the desperate need to make a change, any company who profits from the materialistic and self-centered millennials of China know that a narcissistic self-image is necessary for the bottom line. Advertisers have always wanted us to buy their products, but today, they seem to be sneakier and more capable of reaching out to the most profitable aspects of narcissism.

Materialism

Marketing to tweens (a terms that typically describes girls 8-12 years old) is a $300 billion market. Once people reach adulthood, they may buy a new car every few years, or buy new clothes as new trends come out, but tweens, who are growing and changing physically, cognitively and emotionally *need* new things all the time. Today's tweens require expensive items, like electronics and themed birthday parties. However, nothing is lost on predatory marketers, and now, Kotex makes a line of sanitary napkins specifically for this age group.

Because the money for tween products doesn't come from the target group's pockets, the real market is parents, who are led to believe their kids *need* certain products. This turns out to be relatively easy. In an opinion piece entitled, "Why I allow my daughter to wear THIS" a mother, explaining how her daughter argued and whined her way into a pair of short-shorts from a teen shop, quips "parenthood is all about picking your battles."[63] While this may be good parenting advice, somebody is making billions every time a mom picks her battles. Convincing the parents of boys is probably easier, considering that 68% of parents believe that video games provide an education benefit, brain stimulation,[64] or if nothing else, hand-eye coordination (never mind tossing a ball outside) to their children. Parents of both boys and girls state that safety is the number one reason they bought an expensive cell phone for their child, although every parent I talked to admitted that begging and pleading preceded the big decision. One mom told me that her son needs a phone because using phone and Internet is the way that kids form and strengthen relationships. The media will tell us *anything* to make us spend money!

Of course, not all products marketed to tweens are inherently bad. American Girl, which sells dolls, books, and accessories for young girls pull in millions, and so far, their values have not been questioned. Their books feature girls from a variety of ethnic backgrounds, and their magazine is refreshingly modest, with no beauty, fashion, or romance columns. They also have a line of matter-of-fact, yet age appropriate books that discuss puberty and other problems faced by young girls. However, the cost for an American Girl doll starts at about $100, and does not include the clothes and accessories that most girls want. The company has stores in major metropolitan cities around the county, and their doll-friendly restaurants serve meals for about $35 per person. You can rest assured that American Girl will never sell sex to your daughter, but what they do sell has a price tag that is unattainable for many families living within their means.

Weddings, which once were simply about celebrating marriage, are becoming increasingly narcissistic events. Brides are told over and over *It's all about you…It's your day…whatever you want, you deserve it.* The unrealistic princess fantasies that are now part of modern childhood all but culminate on a woman's special day. Modern weddings are materialistic events, and the marketing slogan "it's your day" sells everything from over-priced dresses to luxury venues. The average wedding in the United States is nearly $30,000. Weddings in other countries are becoming increasingly expensive as well (weddings in China, India and Brazil often cost the same as annual incomes for many families in the same countries), but the focus is different. In other cultures, weddings are about honoring tradition, in the United States, they are about self-expression. Weddings in other cultures celebrate families coming together, religious beliefs being honored and communities being strengthened. American weddings are about the bride and making her feel like a princess or a super model. Wedding pictures, which average about $3,500, are a symbol of the celebrity factor tied into the celebrity experience that modern brides want. Simple posed pictures with family and a wedding cake are not enough. Wedding photos (which replace the engagement photos taken only months before) must look like they came from a magazine. The photographer will airbrush the photos, which is important because they will likely be featured on a photography blog.

Although men are sold a smaller quantity of products than women, the products that define a male status symbol tend to be more expensive. The male status symbol, which often comes down to power more than anything else, is all about accessories, or as many men put it *toys*. Cars, of course, are the old fallback. The car of choice changes from year-to-year, but the car a man drives says a lot about how much money he makes, or more realistically, how much debt he is willing to have.

During college, my best friend, Kristen lived in a small apartment priced right for a poor college student. The building was not fancy, but the car port was filled with expensive cars—BMWs, Mercedes', Audis, and more were more important to their drivers than living in a comfortable home. My husband rides motorcycles, and sometimes co-workers ask for advice on which type to buy. Single men always specify that they want one that will attract women.

Today, technology is rising in importance. Not too long ago, a watch with an expensive logo was the best technology a man owned, today men are more concerned with the phone they use. Apple released the iPhone 5S on September 20, 2013. Hundreds of people slept in line—some for as long as 15 days, so they could be the first to get the gold iPhone. When filmmaker Casey Neistat asked why, almost all of the men (yes, all men) were unsure of their answer, but all seemed proud of how long they were waiting, and proud that their phone would be gold. Each Apple store has a welcome party for the first in line during these events, complete with cheering, applause, and media attention, lest the "winner" forgets how special he is. Two of the men interviewed were professional line-sitters. They get paid to sit in line by people who have the money for hot new items, but can't spare the time to be the first to get them. The other tech gadgets a man can afford to buy represents who he is. Extras, such as boats are also seen as a symbol of wealth and power. Everyone *needs* a car and a house, but only special people *need* boats. Finally, one of the many reasons that women feel so pressured to look perfect (and raise perfect children) is because they themselves are status symbols for their men! That's right, beautiful women are the natural prize for successful men. Several entertainment website and magazines have displayed pictures of beautiful women whose dates are "out of their league." The message is that if a man can land a woman *out of his league*, he must be successful in other ways.

Vanity

Most everything you see on *The Real Housewives of Orange County* is fake. However, the gym where the cast members worked out for many of their early seasons is absolutely real, and real people (like me) also go there to take classes, use equipment , swim and use their amazing showers. Watch out on filming day. Unless you are picture perfect, you will be asked by producers to please move to the back of the class, or even better, off the floor all together. Sorry for the inconvenience, ladies and gentlemen, but our narcissistic reality has no room for *real* reality.

In 2011, Americans spent $10 billion on elective plastic surgery procedures, twice what was spent by NASA on space exploration. No matter what we say, our values are clear. In a narcissistic society, looks are everything. Plastic surgery is so normalized in our culture that in 2009, a plastic surgeon wrote a children's book, geared towards 4-7 year-olds that explains plastic surgery. Considering that the majority of the 12 million cosmetic procedures performed every year are geared toward "fixing" the collateral damage of childbirth (breast augmentations and tummy tucks are among the most popular), there is a real need for a book that can ease the anxiety of a child whose mother undergoes a painful surgery. The side-effect of course is that is sends a loud and clear message to children that our bodies are not good enough. About 18% of cosmetic procedures is done on children ages 13-19. The most common procedures for this age range are breast augmentations in girls, nose jobs, lip and eyelid procedures. Many more teens undergo non-invasive procedures such as tanning, laser hair removal, and Botox injections.[65] An obsession with looks is not limited to girls. Pediatricians have noticed an increase in boys becoming obsessed with gaining muscle. More than 40% of boys as young as twelve exercise regularly to increase muscle mass, almost as many use supplements, and 6% admitted to using steroids at least once (Quick math exercise: If 40% of boys work out to gain muscle, and 32% of boys in the same age range are overweight or obese,[66] only 18% of teen boys adhere to a healthy diet and exercise routine). Steroids are dangerous for anyone, but pose a bigger risk for developing teens who can suffer life-long consequences from disruption to testosterone production.[67]

One problem with this, besides the pressure to look a certain way, is that the results we desire are often unattainable for the average person. Most of our favorite stars have undergone plastic surgery, and by the time we see them in print, they have been heavily air brushed (Cindy Crawford once famously said, "even I don't wake up looking like Cindy Crawford). For all the times in between, celebrities have big bucks to keep up appearances. Jennifer Aniston is rumored to spend over $140,000 a year on beauty (while thousands of women in the 90's didn't understand why their budget salons couldn't get *The Rachel* quite right). Pop singer Rihanna travels with a hair stylist who charges over $3,000 a day, and Princess Kate Middleton spends $3500 on manicures every year. When you add up spray tans, body scrubs, teeth whitening, eyebrow design, botox, and the cost of personal trainers, celebrity beauty costs more than what many families earn in a year. So instead, we spend what we can (and with the help of credit, more than we can) and hope to mimic celebrity looks as much as possible. Expenses that were once unheard of, such as bikini waxes and gym memberships are now the norm for most women.

I have a dear friend who lives in Switzerland, and she was shocked to find that Americans spend money to exercise indoors. In her hometown of Zurich, most families do not own cars, and instead use public transportation and walk. In the United States, the most recent exercise trend, Crossfit, focuses on strength training and costs upwards of $300 a month. Somehow, the Swiss (who have no idea carbs and fat are *bad*) manage to maintain a 6% obesity rate, while Americans, who throw money at beauty, have an obesity rate of 30%.

If you feel good, you look good.

Celiac Disease is a unique autoimmune disorder that affects less than 1% of the population in the United States. Symptoms typically include diarrhea, vomiting, inability to tolerate food, stomach pain and weight loss. The most common treatment for Celiac disease is a gluten-free diet; that is, a diet free of wheat, barley, and rye.[68] Celiac disease is real and painful, and although rare, can create a difficult lifestyle for people forced to adhere to dietary restrictions (gluten is found in most packaged foods, including bread, salad dressings, soy sauce, ice cream, prescription drugs, vitamins and pet food). Recently, a peculiar trend began. Americans, as many as 29%,[69] have begun self-diagnosing and adhering to a gluten-free diet.

Fad diets are nothing new, and have come and gone for decades. Additionally, avoiding certain ingredients is not new. Low fat diets, low sugar diets, low sodium diets, and diets based on plant protein rather than animal proteins, have come, gone and been reinvented time and time again. There are three interesting factors that make the gluten-free craze different than other food crazes. First, unlike avoiding fat, sugar, salt or meat, avoiding gluten provides absolutely no health benefit to the majority of Americans. In fact, plenty of gluten-free foods contain more sugar and fat than the traditional version. Second, the gluten-free food industry is a 4.2 billion dollar operation in the United States, and brings in about $90 million a year in Canada. Adhering to a gluten-free diet is extremely expensive. Even though a gluten-free diet can be maintained by simply eating meat and vegetables, the average gluten-free consumer spends 242-450% more on modified food products that people who buy the traditional version. Grocery giant, Whole Foods Market carries more than 1,000 gluten-free products, including cookies, cakes and pastries, sold at a high premium. Third, in a sea of diet trends, this is the first that has been previously attached to a diet designed to treat a medical disease. The prevalence of celiac disease is less than the prevalence of schizophrenia. Consider that more than twelve million people are living with cancer at any time, ten million more than those living with Celiac. Most Americans don't choose to adhere to a macrobiotic diet, even though years of research have supported its effectiveness in preventing and sometimes treating cancer.

A gluten-free diet does not help people lose weight. In fact, losing weight is a symptom of Celiac disease, not the result of any special diet. So, if there is no health benefit and it is more expensive, why are people going gluten-free?

In an opinion piece about the high cost of shopping at grocery giant Whole Foods, comedienne Kelly MacLean wrote, "Next I see the gluten-free section filled with crackers and bread made from various wheat-substitutes such as cardboard and sawdust. I skip this aisle because I'm not rich enough to have dietary restrictions. Ever notice that you don't meet poor people with special diet needs? A gluten intolerant house cleaner?"[70] At face value, it may seem that food restrictions are a "rich, white person problem" as MacLean puts it, or as I would put it, a sign of rising narcissism, an extension of the need to be *special*. This is complicated and impossible to determine, of course, because although socioeconomic status tends to influence all non-religious food restrictions, it also influences access to health care, and diagnosis of disorders requiring special diets. Plenty of low-income and minority individuals never have the resources to be diagnosed or treated for a plethora of ailments.

The reality lies more in the fact that because the gluten-free diet rarely leads to weight loss, relying less on visible results takes off the pressures. When a person says he is on a gluten-free diet to *feel better* or for general wellness, there is no pressure to fit into small clothes, or more importantly, eat less food. This creates a marketing dream. The gluten-free industry is happy to cater to us, to make us *feel better* about ourselves, by selling us expensive products that most of us don't need, thereby driving up the price for sick people who *are* in need.

Looking good is about more than personal appearance. Once the perfect body, perfect hair and perfect makeup are in place, the material objects are just as important to maintaining the image. Credit inflation, which has allowed people to live the good life without the good income started during the 1990s. During the early

2000s, anyone could buy their dream home. Mortgages were awarded on *stated income*, a system that essentially meant home buyers could "afford" any home they wanted, either by paying interest-only for the first ten years (because of course they will have more money by then) or using one mortgage as a down payment to secure another mortgage. Some homeowners were able to get loans for more than 100% of the home cost, allowing them to remodel or furnish their home. Home developers jumped on board the narcissism train and before long, homes in ordinary neighborhoods were bigger than ever before and boasted features that at one time could only be found in Hollywood mansions.

Now that our hindsight has been adjusted to 20/20, the loans that allowed regular families to go in over their heads are jokingly called NINJA loans (no income, no job, and no assets). At the time, predatory lenders (it wasn't all the consumers' fault, most people still don't understand how mortgage works) did a great job of convincing everyone that these loans would improve neighborhoods by providing pride in ownership and spreading the American dream. Of course, what it really created was ghost towns, destroyed families and a recession. I don't think that an individual is narcissistic simply for taking out a bad loan. However, the narcissism in society sent out the message that owning certain things was tied to self-worth. Further, believing one will be successful, without contingency of hard work or capability is a narcissistic trait. The mortgage industry sold the belief that ordinary people could successfully pay extraordinary loans. The message that we are all entitled makes us believe that *wanting* a large, beautiful home is not enough—we deserve it! Materialism is often an issue for people with true NPD because *having* things and making others jealous is affirming to a person without a healthy sense of self.

Feeling Good. Supporting cancer, specifically breast cancer, has become a marketing campaign to sell products. October is breast cancer awareness month, and every year, companies can count on social media users to spread the word (that is, advertise for free). Of course, awareness *is* extremely important, as early detection and diagnosis save lives. My friend, Regina, who recently won her battle with breast cancer, explained, "I like to promote awareness especially in the month of October. I had no idea what cancer *really* was until I had it. I just wanted to be more aware. I had a symptom long before I was even diagnosed. If I had read about the symptoms I could have caught it long before." The pink ribbons used to promote breast cancer awareness have become increasingly popular in recent years. The intention is to make the public more aware so they can hopefully detect cancer early.

Consumers can buy pink household products. Regina tattooed a pink ribbon on her arm. Although her tattoo is a personal symbol of what she has overcome, there is more to pink ribbons than spreading awareness. Just like the trophies and ribbons handed to children in school and sports, pink ribbons make people *feel good*, as if they made an important contribution to an important cause. Unfortunately, no agency regulates pink ribbons, so any company can put them on any product. Although the average consumer believes that a pink ribbon means the proceeds of a product support breast cancer research, awareness or support, this is not always the case. Some companies use them to indicate a product is "healthy" and does not contribute to breast cancer, others use them to indicate they support breast cancer organizations. All companies who use pink ribbons do so to increase sales.

Even when a company advertises that proceeds of a product will *fight* breast cancer or *benefit* women living with breast cancer, they are not required to indicate how this will be done. Furthermore, many popular pink ribbon campaigns have been promoted by companies whose products are linked to unhealthy habits and even carcinogenic ingredients. For example, in 2008, Yoplait sold yogurt with pink ribbon lids, designed to raise money for breast cancer. At the time, however, the yogurt was made with milk stimulated with rGBH, a hormone linked to cancer. Susan G. Komen for the Cure is one of the biggest offenders. In 2010, the organization was heavily criticized for partnering with fried chicken giant KFC. KFC, known for an unhealthy menu is disproportionately located in low income communities and targets low-income families. A year later, Susan G. Komen for the Cure was involved in the production of a perfume that contained cancer-causing ingredients. The organization pulled their backing in 2012.[71]

One must also ask what it means to support breast cancer awareness and prevention. Susan G. Komen for the Cure, is perhaps the best known breast cancer foundation in the United States. In recent years, they have been the center of criticism and controversy. People throughout the country buy pink ribbon products and participate in runs to support the organization, but they may be funding the foundation's legal team as much as they are funding research. Komen budgets about a million dollars every year for legal fees, and by the end of 2010, had filed legal proceedings against more than 100 small mom-and pop-charities that use the words "for the cure" or the color pink to raise money for cancer research, awareness, or support. These charities are almost always underfunded and unable to hold their ground in court.[72] In 2012, Komen was criticized by members of the pro-choice movement when they decided to eliminate $68,000 in grants to Planned Parenthood. They quickly reversed the decision, upsetting members of the right-to-life movement.[73] Of course, this is an extremely complex issue. As a consumer, I am deeply concerned about the ways that *awareness* is used to make a profit, but as a survivor, Regina says, "I don't have a problem with it. If it raises awareness to one girl that may have cancer, it has a purpose. If the company or charity truly uses its money for prevention, awareness and treatment, it's all worth it."

Feeling Unique, Special and Entitled. My favorite local burger place is a restaurant called Slater's 50/50. Known for their burger made of 50% beef and 50% ground bacon, they also offer a completely customizable burger. The server will hand you a sheet with your options for patty, bread, sauce, cheese and toppings. You fill it out, name the burger something snappy, and hand the sheet back to the server. Before long, the burger, which represents your distinctive taste, is served to you, and announced by name (*The Heather burger is ready!*). Nobody gets hurt from ordering a custom burger (although my cardiologist may disagree) but the belief that buying special, custom products somehow makes us unique is a dangerous narcissistic trend.

Celebrating individual differences is an exciting part of life. As a child, my sister, Hilary and I both had personal items emblazoned with an identical *H* and I resented any gift that involved two identical items—matching dresses, or matching baby dolls, for example. We were different and I wanted our possessions to reflect that. The problem occurs when this natural desire is exploited to sell products. We are told to *express ourselves* and as soon as that idea resonates, we are told what products will make us unique. Once we buy these products, we are just like everyone else and have to buy something else to feel unique again.

Limited offers and exclusive deals are an extension of this need to be special. Although this happens throughout the year, it is especially evident during the holiday season. Back in 1965, Linus in "A Charlie Brown Christmas" was concerned that Christmas was becoming too commercial. What would Linus say if he saw people *fighting* over Christmas gifts? That is exactly what happened in 1983, when physical fights and price-gouging occurred at toy stores across the country. Toy manufacturers caught on quickly, and short-supply toys became the norm, most notably, Tickle Me Elmo, which resulted in physical injuries for store workers and mark-ups as much as six times the retail price. When the Nintendo Wii was released a decade later, at least one man was robbed at gun point after making his exclusive purchase.

Materialism has become more flagrant in recent years. One example is Black Friday sales, which, since the 1960s started the day after Thanksgiving. Retail stores used this day to kick off the holiday season, and offer exclusive deals on a very limited quantity of specific products. Initially, most Black Friday sales started around 6am, but throughout the years, started earlier and earlier. In 2011, several major retailers opened at midnight, and in 2012, many sales began at 8pm Thanksgiving Day. By 2013, several retailers, including Kmart and Wal-Mart, were open all of Thanksgiving Day. This was a problem for many because low-paid retail workers were required to return to work on Thanksgiving Day, before the turkey was cold. By

2013, many retailers opted to open on Thanksgiving as normal, or earlier. More frightening, however, was the behavior of people intent on the unique honor of saving $100 on a laptop. In 2008, more than 2,000 people broke down the door of a Long Island Walmart five minutes before it was scheduled to open. An employee was killed, and another employee who tried to help was seriously injured. The crowd continued to push past paramedics and police. On the same night, two men shot each other to death in a crowded Toys R Us store in California. Both men died in front of their children, as well as hundreds of frightened witnesses. In 2011, a Los Angeles woman began pepper spraying Walmart shoppers over video games. These are not isolated incidents, and people are injured or even killed over toys each year.

Although savings comes with these purchases, they are not substantial for most shoppers. The average Black Friday savings is about 30%, and the average shopper spends about $300 during the spree. People are not trampling each other to save less than $100. A person who is truly struggling could shop online (Cyber Monday deals typically offer better savings), buy used products, or simply buy more affordable gifts. Remember, people with NPD feel special and unique, and also feel above the law. I know for a fact that not everyone who shops on Black Friday has NPD, but getting a good deal on a special item makes shoppers feel unique and special. Additionally, the act of pushing, shoving or trampling another human being for material items is a display of malignant entitlement. Some have argued that fighting and competing is part of human nature. After all, all mammals naturally try to establish dominance. The Japanese, however, who are known for being polite and orderly, had no problem maintaining composure after their country was ravaged by a tsunami in 2011. There was no rioting, looting, violence, or price-gouging for basic supplies. Citizens who had just lost everything, including loved ones, waited patiently in line for provisions. If Japan can get through a national state of emergency with compassion and ethics intact, human nature should not get in the way of Christmas shopping.

Part 3

THE NARCISSISTIC INDIVIDUAL

Chapter 7

NARCISSISM IN
RELATIONSHIPS

---

*"I cry, cry, cry
Then I complain
Come back for more
Do it again"*

– Rilo Kiley, *Glendora*

*"Women cannot complain about men anymore
until they start getting better taste in them."*
– Bill Maher

There is no polite way to ask. Carrie has been married to a narcissist for 21 years. She is pretty, with whimsical style that makes her look like a cross between Helena Bonham Carter and Stevie Nicks. She is smart, educated and articulate. She doesn't seem like the type of woman to ever be trapped in an unhappy marriage or put up with nonsense. There is no polite way to ask, so I just ask, "Why did you stay in the relationship?"

This isn't a new question for Carrie. Maybe she's been asked, or just asked herself. Maybe she has hashed it out in therapy over the years or with friends during one of multiple marital hiatuses. Carrie responds with a carefully constructed answer, that is glaringly absent of specific examples from her own life.

"Being in a relationship with a narcissist involves low self-esteem and the resultant lack of motivation to improve one's self or one's life. *I do not deserve a more mutually reciprocal and thus, satisfying relationship so I get to whine about this one. I am stuck here in this relationship so I cannot lose weight, seek help for depression, get a better job, make my dreams come true or worse yet, even contemplate what they may be.* If children are involved, having one narcissistic parent creates a situation where the other parent's life is monopolized by attending to the children's needs because the narcissist does not consider many needs besides his own. This allows the non-narcissist to feel even more needed, sacrificing, self-pitying and important which discourages the non-narcissist from asking for help. If I ask for help, I may not get it. If I get help, I cannot play the victim. The partner of a narcissist must derive pleasure—consciously, unconsciously, sub-consciously, hero syndrome, martyr syndrome, people pleaser, rescuer, need for drama, past life issues. *I am happiest when I am overcompensating, People will love me if I am a helping*—which makes staying in a painful relationship more perversely satisfying than ending one."

Carrie has also considered the complex factors that attract people to narcissists. She explains that her idea relates to the Imago Theory. "This involves having at least one emotionally distant parent thus, as a child, the non-narcissist is constantly trying, trying, trying to capture that parent's attention, feel secure in that parent's continual affection, and receive that parent's approval. This quest is most likely going to be unsuccessful. Therefore, as a teen and young adult, the non-narcissist seeks a similarly challenging potential partner through which she or he can pursue and obtain what was lacking in childhood, to fill the absent parent-sized hole. Likewise and despite all the emotional torment, this quest is equally unsuccessful and builds anger, hurt and resentment toward the narcissist for really just being who he/she is and for not being whom the other partner desperately needs him or her to be. Of course, it is unfair to expect either partner to heal the other's childhood wounds." Carrie believes that the non-narcissist feels noble for continuing to love the narcissist.

When Carrie began to tell me her story, it was clear that her theory was based on her own experiences. She explained that she had had many romantic relationships in which she gave more than her partner and accepted much less than she deserved.

She confessed, "My slide into compliance in adult life seemed natural since I grew up in a home where adult needs, issues, and concerns overrode mine. Until around age 13, I did not recognize that I had needs. I remember always having to be good and not upset the apple cart. This was made even more apparent when my parents divorced. Mom went back to college, began teaching elementary school again, took care of our house and raised my older sister and me. It felt as if everything was dumped on her and it was and she reminded us of that frequently. I felt as if I were a burden and submerged my own needs even more.

"My maternal grandparents would come from Iowa and stay for elongated visits which I enjoyed as I loved them a great deal and vice versa. They became another set of parents in many ways and helped my mother take care of us and our home. They gave us things my mother could not. But simultaneously, they threatened my sister and me that if we did not behave, we would upset our grandfather who already had had one ulcer and worse, they may return to Iowa and, God forbid, we make anything worse for our mom. The mantra was that our *dad did not care about us. He left and did not care if our car did not work or if we had clothes or food or...* This warning was delivered after some typical sibling argument my sister and I might have or perhaps we did not show appreciation for whatever was being served or did not do somersaults about going over to some old folks' house for three hours to "visit" which really meant sit in a chair and try not to die of boredom in the middle of the Hummel-filled living room. I learned that we were not to make any form of waves. I could entertain them, go with whatever they decided the flow was and color only within the lines. Despite all that was positive, this was a form of emotional blackmail."

These experiences made Carrie terrified to assert herself or ask for any of her needs to be met. She remembers that her grandfather regularly chewed Juicy Fruit gum. Once, a few nights before he was scheduled to return to Iowa, her sister asked him for a piece of gum. Carrie was shocked. How could she dare express a need so openly? Of course, she was given the gum without incident, but Carrie remained amazed by her impertinence. In Carrie's mind, her young sister had clearly crossed the invisible line. "Are you crazy? You don't ask for gum! More than 40 years later, I only now realize this was beyond ridiculous."

Throughout college, Carrie dated and slept around a little. She says, "It was casual and fun, mutually disconnected. However, if I was serious about someone, I would allow myself to be put into compromised situations. One winter quarter, there was this big gorgeous boy in my Chaucer class. He gave me a Valentine and soon he was a genuine prospect. I invited him over for dinner. The food, table and I were wonderful. He told me he loved me that night and I believed him because I wanted to so badly. That may have been good news except in the same breath; he told me he loved two other girls too. I somehow did not hear the second part of the statement and even if I had, I figured I could easily win him over so he'd dump the competition. Big surprise, he did not and I kept at him and at him until we hated each other. It tore me apart. A healthy non-desperate woman would have said at the beginning *Oh, you love me? Well isn't that great? But sorry, pal, I am not going to have to share anyone. I am better than that. If you love me, you can love only me. I am not interested in being a member of your harem.* He ended up marrying one of the girls, not both though, that I know of."

When Carrie was 26, she had a significant relationship with a man whom she felt was perfect for her. They fell in love quickly and she assumed this would lead to marriage, children, and true life *happily ever after*. His family owned a restaurant, where he was expected to work most nights. She spent every weekend with him at the restaurant, figuring he would propose. He never did. She says, "He wanted me when it was convenient for him. He wanted monogamy but not a long term commitment and I foolishly obliged mislead by folly. I would talk about marriage and children and he remained silent. Hmmm, a red flag I did not want to see! Why did I not explain to him that this arrangement was not acceptable? Why didn't I feel I deserved more? That I would no longer tolerate this relationship operating on his terms? He could either commit or let me go. Meanwhile, many friends my age were getting married, having children. How could they be so lucky while I was stuck in limbo and not deserving of those grand life events? I was just the weekend girlfriend. A few years of this and I became bitter, difficult which pushed him further away."

Carrie and her boyfriend eventually broke up and she was spun into a serious depression that lasted nearly two years. Her energy and concentration were so low she had to take a leave of absence from graduate school. She went to bed every night hoping to die before she could wake up. She went to therapy but did not find it helpful. She explains, "I existed in a fog. No friends, no family—nothing but me, my job and a cat pee-smelling, poorly air-conditioned apartment on a noisy street. In the late '80's—anti-depressants were not given out like breath mints as they are now but finally I did see a psychiatrist and began taking Prozac. I felt *saved* immediately, hopeful—like my old self again. I was happy, a little manic even. I felt that all my good qualities were shining like beacons. I could do this life thing again. I had been to hell and crawled back. I had earned my stripes and then I met Lucas, my current husband of 21 years, father of my two daughters."

Lucas was a substitute at the high school where Carrie was an English teacher. When I asked how they met, she explained, "I had noticed him when he was around—friendly, sexy, a bit cocky—the bad boy type. I liked the way he walked in his tight jeans and cowboy boots. We were introduced by a mutual acquaintance. He came to my classroom one lunch. He asked me for my phone number as we walked but did not write it down so I was surprised when he really did call to set up our first date. It did not seem as much as a date as it did a therapy session for him. I was the mature, self-supporting, responsible, intelligent, attentive, compassionate, supportive one and he spoke about how he was sick of the bar scene, basically unsatisfied with one night stands. He did not like being a sub. He did not want to be an actor despite his degree in theater. He was clearly afloat compared to me who seemed well-anchored."

Carrie was still recovering from her depression and not interested in starting a serious relationship. Still, they went on a few dates and had a good time. One night he pulled into her driveway after a night of drinking and flashed his headlights into her apartment window. She told him that she was sleeping and he did not believe her. He began insisting that she had another man in her apartment. "He would not go away. Instead of my feeling that his behavior was presumptuous and controlling, I was flattered by it. I let him into my apartment and into my heart. Problem was he really did not know what to do. We lived for years with him still wanting his drinking and partying life; and me waiting at home alone." Lucas went to Laughlin with his friends instead of being with Carrie on her 30th birthday. He would borrow her car to play golf and leave Carrie waiting. For a multitude of emotional reasons, she put up with it and continued loving him. "One night he went out drinking with his cousins and called me around 2 am from a Del Taco drive-thru. I had no idea he'd stay out so late but when he did finally stumble home, I told him that I was so happy he came home to me. I vomit a bit now when I think of that."

Despite Carrie's desire for marriage and family, nothing changed. He continued to go out with his friends when he wanted, and spent time with Carrie on his own terms. She describes feeling as though she came second to his friends and that if they didn't approve of her, he would take that as a negative reflection of himself and his taste in women. "I had to be fun enough even though by then I was not much of a party girl and hated drunken bullshit talk. I cooked, cleaned, spoiled him, brought him presents—all that crap. We had been together for two years when we went shopping for rings. I think he did love me and felt he should marry me—but I do not think he was the type of person who wanted to be married, who wanted to settle down and have a committed relationship." His proposal was delivered in a left turn lane as they drove back from a jewelry store. Looking back, Carrie believes she should have taken the rings and tossed them out the truck's window. "I should have gotten out, slammed the door and kept on walking. *That's how you propose? That crappy gesture is all I am worth?* But no, I set about planning the wedding, all aglow."

Carrie and Lucas were married. For their honeymoon, they took a cruise to the Mexican Riviera. She explains that she continued to notice negative quirks. "One was that he was clearly uncomfortable when we were on the pool deck. I could tell that it was because I am not the kind of woman who can sport a string bikini. Granted, 21 years ago, I looked better in a swimsuit than now, but that still was not good enough. I made him self-conscious. When we ate dinner, he talked and talked and talked and talked to the couple we were assigned to eat with and even agreed to hang out with them in Mazatlán. Rather than focusing on me, he and the other guy did tequila shots which resulted in his being sick and me being stuck with him in one of those teeny rooms. Fun. Before we dropped anchor in Cabo, I wanted to throw his vomiting self overboard."

They made their way home and eventually bought their first house. His drinking and time spent away continued to cause problems between them and before long, Lucas drifted into fundamental Christianity. Lucas's new religious commitment did temporarily help him control his alcoholism, but Carrie saw it as a simple switch to a new addiction. "I wanted no part in his new obsession. While not an atheist by any stretch, I do not accept many fundamentalist beliefs. To me, they are often ignorant and arrogant. He continued on in this for about a year during which he told me I'd be going to hell because I was not *saved*. His fervor waned with time and after we'd had our first daughter."

At this point in her story, Carrie stopped abruptly. "Pretty much I could go on and on with this selfish act and that inconsiderate choice, 23 years of them, but I did marry him, stay with him, buy a home with him, have two children with him and so on." The essence of Carrie's story is that no matter what, Lucas will always think of himself first. She does give him some credit. Carrie admits that that when she points out a problem, he readily apologizes, a quality he did not possess a decade ago. She says, "In a lot of ways, he is a reformed narcissist, meaning his first reaction is to protect or watch out for himself, but now I can point this out to him and he will listen. I think he learned to listen and not defend himself or he will do that initially and then sure enough, if I wait he changes his tune." And she ends with a point that is true in most difficult marriages, "Just because you divorce someone, especially the father of your children, he will remain part of your life and hopefully, a beneficial part of his children's lives. If our situation had not challenged him to change, he probably would not have." Still, as she explains, "it wastes a lot of energy and likewise I am always expecting some form of disappointment or hurt. I have grown used to it. It often feels like the grooves have been so worn, that so many hurts have been piled upon so many hurts that there will never be a fresh start or clean slate and I have grown tired of always watching my emotional back."

Romance and Narcissistic Charm

The only part of Carrie's story that is atypical, is that she and Lucas are still married after 23 years together. The personality traits and recurring conflict are extremely common to a relationship that involves a narcissist. As difficult as Carrie's life has been, falling in love with a narcissist is easy. Narcissists are charming. They know how to please others and can easily compliment and express desire. Studies have found that high narcissistic traits are correlated with higher levels of charm, physical attractiveness, humor, and interpersonal warmth.[74]

Narcissists make a potential partner feel desired. Individuals with NPD may plan extravagant dates or give expensive gifts. Eva, a woman who divorced a narcissistic husband after a 5 year marriage shared the story of an early date. "I was living in Boston for college when we met. During our second date, I told him about my favorite hamburger place back in L.A. Within an hour, we were at the airport and he was buying tickets so we could get a burger and come back in time for my classes later in the week."

What's more, partners of narcissists often feel a really strong chemistry, as if the relationship is meant to be. In fact, several studies[74] have found that men with narcissistic traits (not necessarily a NPD diagnosis) have an easier time meeting women. Narcissists come across as confident and charming, traits that successfully attract women. Once the relationship is established, however, red flags start to appear. The partner of a person with NPD often describes the experience as exhausting. A person with NPD needs a very high level of attention and can alternate clingy and aloof behavior at different times. Narcissists are hard to please. Because they have so few boundaries, they readily point out their partner's deficiencies. When the partner without NPD tries to discuss hurt, disappointment, or a bad day, the narcissistic partner is quick to point out personal faults that may have caused the problem.

The partner without NPD may become embarrassed of her partner for typical NPD behaviors. A person with NPD is likely to cut in line, be rude to a waitress, or behave in entitled ways. Emily, a young woman who married a narcissist right out of high school described the first time she was embarrassed by his rude behavior. "We were looking for parking in Hollywood and a woman was loading shopping bags and two small children into her car. David wanted the parking spot, so he drove up really close and started honking and yelling for her to hurry up. The poor woman was doing the best she could. He started yelling at *me* when I told him he was being rude. I was so angry at him; I got out of the car and began walking away from him. When he finally found me, he apologized with tears in his eyes, telling me he loved me and was terrified of losing me."

Because people with NPD are extremely sensitive, emotional discussions can be very difficult. When told that their behavior is embarrassing, hurtful or rude, they become defensive. Because shame is at the core of the narcissistic personality, narcissistic behavior is often shameless. People with NPD are rarely sorry for their bad behavior. Unless that are actively trying to manipulate a partner, a person with NPD may be slow to apologize. Even when not trying to manipulate another person, the narcissist lacks empathy and cannot see his partner's point of view. This makes relational communication and problem solving nearly impossible. Similarly, many people with NPD express sadness or hurt as anger or rage.

Narcissism and Sex

Sexuality is a common tool used by narcissists of both sexes. In his article Love, Sex and Marriage in the Setting of Pathological Narcissism, researcher Salman Akhatar[75] explains the seven stages necessary for a healthy sexual relationship. The first step is subtle hints or flirting that indicates sexual readiness. Next is initial physical foreplay while dressed, such as kissing. Undressing and more direct sexual foreplay is followed by sexual intercourse. Orgasm comes next, followed by post-coital intimacy, such as cuddling or talking. The final stage is transition back into non-sexual behavior, which can include dressing, sleeping, or talking about non-sexual issues. A person with either NPD or narcissistic traits may face problems during any of these stages. As for the early stages, the narcissist sees his own needs first and may not be concerned with subtle hints from a potential partner. Similarly, he may make overt sexual advances rather than the subtle flirtations common in our culture. Because the narcissist seeks control and desires to be desired, narcissists of both sexes may choose to ignore the subtle signals given by another person in order to increase desirability or withhold affection. This can create confusion for the other person, especially when a romantic relationship has already been established.

Narcissists, particularly men, tend to skip over foreplay when possible. Out of a disregard for his partner's needs, the narcissist may move too quickly toward the next stage. From an evolutionary perspective, foreplay serves an important purpose. The process of removing clothing and offering one's nakedness to another is a process of overcoming shame and building trust, which is necessary for a healthy romantic relationship. Problems with trust, disinterest in forming an emotionally tight relationship, and insecurity over physical appearance may cause a narcissist to avoid foreplay. Conversely, some narcissistic men may attempt to hide their discomfort by serving their partner's needs, typically with oral sex. This may create the appearance of being a very giving lover without exposing his own body. Greedy by nature, the narcissist may confuse his partner when he switches from being very sexually giving to wanting to take. Both narcissistic men and women prefer sexual positions with limited face-to-face contact. Likewise, both men and women with NPD have trouble achieving orgasm, typically because of their inability to give up control and self, even if for just a moment. This often results in narcissistic women faking orgasm and men bragging about how long they can last.

The final two stages of the sexual experience are also difficult for the narcissist. After orgasm, many couples enjoy time together, even if for only a short while. The narcissist is uncomfortable with post-coital chat, eye contact and cuddling. The transition back into non-sexual behavior is also a challenge. For these reasons, the sexual experience may end abruptly, or sexual behavior, talk, and innuendo may continue into post-sexual activities and conversation.

When in a relationship, the narcissist may become sexually bored. This boredom may be overcome by trying new positions, toys, or partners. Many narcissists, particularly men, avoid exclusive relationships. They may express feeling "trapped" when the relationship comes to a point where monogamy is expected. When men with NPD do marry, often it is out of obligation to the image they are trying to portray. Unfaithfulness is a common and serious problem is narcissistic relationships. Although variations occur across sexes, females with NPD are more likely to see marriage as a tool for further control or self-benefit.

Narcissists often see sexual conquests as challenges that will make them more desirable. They are quick to brag about their sexual encounters and many narcissists look for challenging sexual relationships. Narcissistic men, for example, may seek out lesbians, virgins or married women and feel as though they have accomplished something after the sexual act has occurred.

Julia sought therapy to deal with feelings she was experiencing after an extramarital affair. She and Rob had worked together for five years, and after she left work to stay home with her two children, he began sending her flirty text messages. "It started innocently enough, but after a while, the texts became more sexually explicit. I wasn't physically attracted to him, but I loved the attention. We saw each other at few social functions, and every chance he had when nobody was looking, he would touch me in a forbidden way. It was really exciting. I loved my husband and our marriage was great. Maybe it was because I turned 40 that year, but I felt like I really needed the attention." Julie and Rob flirted for nearly three years before they had opportunity to consummate the relationship. "When he finally came over for sex, it was the worst sexual encounter of my life. It was extremely awkward and reminded me of high school. The moment he finished, he disappeared into my bathroom to clean up, as if I wasn't even there. Within minutes, he was dressed and walking out the door. Because I didn't want a relationship with him, I expected it to be casual as detached, but I didn't expect to feel so used."

Even though Julie did not enjoy it, she began feeling guilty as if she had made a mistake during the encounter. "Instead of feeling guilty for betraying my husband, I kept thinking of everything I did wrong with Rob and what I could have done differently. He had asked me to do something in bed that just felt *wrong* at the time. I thought I would have a chance to do it another time. In the days and weeks after, I kept wishing I had just done it." Julie was surprised when she stopped hearing from Rob. "He texted me almost every day for three years and he suddenly stopped. I wanted to talk to him, but was trying to not appear desperate. I was confused, because I wanted to keep it light and fun. I had no intention of leaving my husband, and he was married, too. I didn't want him to love me or even date me. Even though he used me and walked out on *me*, I wanted another opportunity to prove myself to him, to show him that we could have fun together." Julie was able to control herself from contacting Rob, but she fantasized about "righting" their encounter by seducing him until she was in a deep depression.

It is impossible to diagnose Rob as having NPD based on Julie's experience with him. Rob isn't the first man to use a woman sexually, and Julie clearly has self-esteem and marital issues outside of her relationship with Rob. Still, Rob's sexual behaviors during their encounter and his treatment of Julie afterward, are common displays of narcissistic traits in relationships. Many narcissists feel validated just knowing that somebody else finds them sexually attractive. Narcissists also tend to have shallow attachments to others. Julie and Rob had been friends for eight years and he had no problem detaching completely after a single sexual encounter. In addition to feeling sexually rebuffed, Julie was mourning a friendship that she valued. Julie's extreme confusion over her own feelings and her place with Rob is familiar among women in relationships with narcissists.

Narcissistic Women

When discussing narcissism in relationships, it is easy to assume that the narcissist is a man. Although the majority of people diagnosed with NPD are male, female narcissists can also wreak havoc on relationships. Narcissistic traits are the same in both sexes, but can be manifested differently in relationships. Narcissism in women is very similar to Borderline Personality Disorder (BPD), which is characterized by an intense fear of abandonment, which typically involves narcissistic-like manipulations. Like with women who fall in love with BPD men, a man is roped in by the intense chemistry he feels with his BPD mate. The sex is usually fantastic and he feels wanted. A woman with BPD may watch a man for a long time before approaching, so she already knows quite a bit about him. She may also show up unexpected, as if she randomly ran into her love interest. Like men with NPD, women with BPD are critical and difficult to please. Women with BPD are also manipulative and controlling.

Brody was in his early 30s when he met Jamie. He had dated very infrequently and was flattered when Jamie fell so quickly in love. Within six weeks of their first meeting, she had moved into his house, where he let her live for free so she could get her commercial debt under control. Shortly after she moved in, Jamie had posted on the refrigerator a 6-page list of things she wanted to change about Brody's house and Brody himself. One day he came home from work, and his sofa had been sold because she didn't like it. Before long, Brody had stopped seeing his friends and quit softball, which he had played every week for the past four years. Jamie insisted that he visit her parents with her every weekend, even though they lived in a different state. Jamie was controlling every aspect of his life. Brody was really confused. In some ways, he was really unhappy. Jamie would blow up and Brody didn't understand why. She had frequent temper tantrums or silence spells and Brody was never sure what set her off. On the other hand, Brody was so happy to finally be in a relationship. He was so desperate for sex that he justified his troubles as just being part of an adult relationship. When Brody and Jamie were married, several friends shared concerned over the relationship. Jamie decided not to invite them to the wedding, further isolating Brody.

Another tactic commonly employed by narcissistic women is gaslighting. This involves creating a tense or unhappy situation and then behaving as though unaware. The narcissist will build trust, then tear it down. Jamie, for example, would withhold sex without any apparent reason or explanation. She would pull away at Brody's touch and go days without talking. When he would respond she would say,

"What's wrong? I don't know what you're talking about." A similar tactic is to provoke anger with sarcasm and snide comments, then act confused when the partner responds with anger or emotion.

Narcissism in Same Sex Relationships

Very little research has examined narcissism in gay and lesbian couples. It is widely assumed that the relationship challenges are similar to those faced by heterosexual couples. Classic Freudian psychoanalytic theory suggested that homosexuality itself was the ultimate narcissistic act because it allowed the narcissist to have sex with a partner more similar to himself. Until the 1970s, homosexuality and narcissism were rarely viewed as separate issues. Although understanding of homosexuality has come a long way in the past century, studies of college students have found that gay men have higher levels of narcissistic traits and lower self-esteem than their heterosexual peers.[76] Today, environmental theories aim to explain the connection between homosexuality and narcissism. This view speculates that narcissistic traits develop in response to the oppressive nature of an overwhelmingly heterosexual society. A similar view is that the gay community has high expectations for the physical appearance of men and narcissistic traits are an adaptive response to this pressure. Because all research to date on this subject involves college aged men, many believe that the narcissist traits reflect maturity or the development of identity, not sexuality itself.[77] Even less is known about narcissism in lesbian relationships, probably because narcissism is a predominantly male disorder.

Leaving a Narcissist

Erica has been divorced for 18 months. Every morning, she wakes up to a text message from her ex-husband, Jason. The messages begin early in the day and continue until she goes to bed. Then they start again. She explains that since she stopped responding over a year ago, he goes through full cycles that range from love to rage. Each cycle starts with him professing his love and begging to her to come back and mend their family. Sometimes, he asks for sex. Other times, he tells her that he is very ill and needs her help. He has faked cancer three times since their divorce. Before long, the messages become threatening. He threatens to take the kids or make her life difficult financially. Eventually, he apologizes and the cycle begins again. Erica has been living in a borrowed camping trailer with her three children because it is easier than life with Jason.

When Erica first met Jason, there was instant chemistry. She feels shallow now, believing that the attraction was mostly sexual. Erica is a self-described dead head, and at the time, Jason was the most stable man she knew. He had an impressive work ethic and took pride in his sales career. At 26, she was looking for security and she says, "he was a dead head who had his shit together." She also enjoyed being desired. "It was like a caveman hitting a woman over the head with a club and saying *I want you.*" Erica attributed Jason's inflated ego to his career in sales. She said that being a big shot was important to him and he treated others in a way that reflected this. He had a strong network of influential friends, and even with only a 9th grade education, he was able to achieve success. Jason refused to do mundane work or anything he felt was beneath him. For example, he refused to do clerical work or log his hours. When confronted by management, he pointed out his successes and the money he had earned for the company.

Jason started to get difficult and controlling about two months into the relationship. She explained that he became angry when she exhibited behaviors that illuminated his deficiencies. For example, Jason's social anxiety made him unable to attend her cousin's wedding. He became enraged when Erica wanted to attend without him. They fought over the issue for hours. Looking back, Erica wishes she had been able to see how ridiculous it was. She says, "I hate that I was that stupid. The relationship shouldn't have lasted more than a year." Jason exerted control over every area of Erica's life. He forced her to back out of a trip to Europe she planned with her girlfriends. Erica explained that in each of Jason's tirades, he made one true point and she believed the sacrifices he was asking her to make "is what you do when you settle down."

After they were married, Erica went back to school to earn her master's degree in education. She says that this was bragging rights for Jason. "He was so proud of how smart and educated I was, he bragged about it to everyone." Erica confided that her worst memory during this time in her life was their evening phone calls. Erica taught school during the day and took classes at night. Jason called her every day as she drove home and engaged her in phone sex.

As a stay at home mom of two small children, Erica enjoyed a weekly support group for moms. During one session, she shared that she loved being a mother but did not enjoy being a wife. The concerned group leader talked to Erica privately. One of the problems Erica was experiencing at the time was that Jason had an intense need for attention every morning upon waking. In addition to pressing sexual needs, she described that he was clingy and didn't understand that she needed to care for the children and couldn't give him the attention he wanted. He became whiny and threw a tantrum when she attended to their newborn instead of him. After talking for several minutes, the group leader suggested that his behavior seemed narcissistic. This was the first time that Erica had ever shared Jason's behavior with another person and had that person reflect back with disgust.

Erica had been with Jason 10 years when her younger sister confessed that Jason had been hitting on her. Erica still doesn't know exactly what happened between the two, but she knows they had an inappropriate flirtatious relationship and that he sent her sister text messages at night after she fell asleep. Erica took the children and went to her mother's house. She says, "For the first time, I had an intense clarity. I saw him for what he was for the first time." Still, she wasn't ready to leave. She wanted to fix the relationship and Jason agreed to go to marriage therapy. A few months into their reconciliation, Erica was pregnant with their third child. During her third pregnancy, Erica cut Jason off sexually. She remembers he became meaner as he was unable to cope. She was ready to leave, but needed time after the baby was born.

Erica and Jason worked hard in marriage therapy. Erica did not want to lose their marriage and Jason did not want to lose Erica. A few months into therapy, their psychologist suggested that Jason may have Asperger's syndrome (AS). Jason became hyper-focused on researching AS. After pouring over books and websites, he believed it was a perfect fit. Erica also felt it helped to explain some of his controlling and anxious behaviors. For example, Jason was a sex addict. She explains that he became obsessed and "had a fetish of the week." She felt like this could be part of the narrow interests often displayed by those with AS. People with AS are often goal oriented and can be insensitive to others, especially when trying to achieve a specific goal. Equipped with this diagnosis, Erica and Jason saw a psychiatrist. Jason was prescribed anti-depressants and anti-anxiety medications. Erica says that after that "Jason used his diagnosis as an excuse for everything." Still, this seemed like a reasonable explanation and Erica forgot about the possibility of narcissism.

The diagnosis and the therapy was not enough to repair Erica's marriage. Their sexual relationship became more complicated and Erica became more confused and unhappy. She says the last year and a half of their marriage was "all about the kids. I had to be OK with the decision to break up my family. I never thought I would be the kind of person who got divorced. I never thought I could do that to my family." Erica woke up one morning knowing that she needed to leave. Once again, she took her children and moved in with her mother. "I told him he had one more opportunity to change but I was not going to live with him while he did it. He never took the opportunity. He is not capable of doing what a normal man is capable of when losing his family."

During her divorce, Erica discussed some of her problems with a friend. Her friend grew up with narcissistic father and her entire family was torn part while her mother spent eight years trying to divorce. She worked in technology and knew several adults with

AS. She explained some fundamental differences between AS and narcissism. For one, a person with AS may be insensitive and rigid, but they never intentionally hurt those they love. Narcissists, on the hand, are intentionally manipulative. Although narcissists and people with AS both experience social anxiety, narcissists like Jason are able to fit into social situations for their own benefit. Jason's success in sales was attributed to his ability to be a social chameleon. People with AS also don't have the sense of entitlement that Jason displayed. Like Jason, a person with AS may refuse to make cold calls or learn new technology, but out of routine, not because they feel they are too good to do the work.

Since their split, Jason has showed very little interest in the couple's three young children. Erica wanted her children to have a father in their life, but his flaking, bullying and harassment made it difficult. She is planning to move out of state as soon as possible and take her children with her. She worries a little that her children, particularly her 7-year-old son may resent her for this choice someday. However, she knows that Jason's relationship with the children is very unhealthy. He engages with the children very little, but when he does, he lays heavy emotional adult issues on them. Just last week, she overheard her 3-year-old daughter give him tips for being less lonely.

Why Not Just Leave?

Leaving a narcissist is hard work. First, a person with NPD is capable of switching on the charm that led to the initial attraction. Although narcissists are not necessarily physically abusive, the cycle tends to be similar to the abuse cycle. A typical abuse cycle begins with the honeymoon phase. During this phase, the abuser is respectful, apologetic for past behavior, and seems happy and loving. Next comes the tension phase. This phase is a time when insults, threats, and mood swings build up. After that, the explosion phase comes with overtly abusive behavior, which can range from intimidating body language and name calling, or hitting and sexual assault. For the narcissist, the honeymoon phase is similar. The narcissist uses all the tactics that were used to start the relationship. Gifts, compliments, personal time spent together, and over-the-top apologies often smooth over past transgressions. Then, things get tense. Narcissistic traits become more apparent. Finally, the final straw occurs. Depending on the couple, this could be any number of behaviors. Rude behaviors to a loved one, missing an important event, or even an affair start the cycle all over again. Of course, a narcissist can be physically or sexually abusive to a partner, which makes the relationship even more painful, confusing and difficult for the partner.

Another reason leaving a narcissist is difficult is because even when the charm is turned off behind closed doors, the outside world still sees a happy, energetic person. The friends and family of the narcissist's partner may find stories of bad behavior confusing and work to justify the transgression, no matter how serious. Just as women who are physically abused feel isolated, the narcissist's partner becomes isolated. The partner of a person with NPD may be afraid to get help because friends and family may say "it can't be that bad" or minimize the experience. Narcissists are master manipulators and thrive on manipulating others for their own benefit. Many couples try marriage counseling before deciding to divorce. Although this can be helpful, the narcissist often feels a lack of control during counseling. He or she tends to believe that the therapist sides with the spouse and may want to try several therapists or disengage entirely, believing that all exercises and suggestions are a personal attack.

Narcissists are some of the most difficult people to divorce. Divorce, by its nature is an emotional battle for anyone. It represents an extreme loss, and for many people, a failure. These feelings are even more intense for the narcissist because they present a threat to his grandiose self-image and his control over his life, his partner, and his children.[78] Infidelity is a common problem among narcissists, and even when caught, the narcissist will fight for his marriage to keep his sense of self intact. Because the narcissist has no emotional ties to extramarital partners, he justifies his affairs and is genuinely surprised and hurt when his wife will not tolerate the behavior. The narcissist will go great lengths to keep his marriage intact. He will turn on the charm he used to initiate the relationship and he will beg. He will also use his children. A common tactic is to ask for family activities, for the purpose of not disrupting the children. "I know we aren't together, but can we take the kids to the zoo?" or "We should have Thanksgiving as a family, for the children."

In previous generations, it was typical for women to gain custody of children after a divorce. Today, family law courts strive for an equal arrangement, and anything less than ideal is a threat to the narcissistic father. The divorce process will likely set a narcissist on a destructive path to quickly regain—either by denial, inflation, distortion or negation—the sense of self that was destroyed in the divorce.

When children are involved, the easiest way for a narcissistic man to regain control over his former wife is to use the children as tools. This is often done through litigation. A narcissist will sue for custody, even unreasonable custody. It is also common for a narcissist to try to prove that the other parent, usually the mother in these cases, is unfit. The narcissistic parent may try to alienate the other parent, by seeking third party "witnesses" to testify on his behalf or against the other parent. The narcissist's struggle to gain custody is often done with little regard for the children's routines. Common examples include wanting to pull the children out of school, or wanting visitation that interferes with scout meetings or sports. The narcissistic parent will do everything to keep the child from the other parent. This serves to cut off the child's contact with the other parent, and also protects the narcissist from any allegations that may come from the child's communication with the other parent. An alienated child can easily be manipulated into defending a narcissistic parent. It is also common for visitation with children to slowly wane. The narcissist will have an arsenal of excuses, blaming the court system, the child's mother, or the children themselves. A common situation is to contact the mother, saying that the child is rude or disrespectful during visits because of the way she is raising the child in his absence. With older children it is common to say that the child is pushing him away, or prefers to be with friends.[78] It is easy to say that such statements made by narcissists are lies. In truth, they are distorted realities and exaggerations of self-worth. The narcissist also feels genuinely attacked by his spouse and the court system. The narcissist, unequipped to meet his child's emotional needs, must reframe the truth in a way that protects his view of himself.

Who is Attracted to a Narcissist?

As discussed earlier, anyone can be initially attracted to a narcissist. Narcissists are typically attractive, fun, and have a great sense of humor. However, the initial charm usually wears off after about four months[74] and most people in relationships with a narcissist will leave, even if they are hurt and bewildered by the experience. Because men are more likely than women to appreciate short-term relationships, they are less likely to be bothered by the dynamics of a relationship with a narcissist. Specific traits in women can make them more likely to stay in a relationship with a man with narcissistic traits. Women with a "caretaking" personality, for example, are prone to wanting to work on the relationship and stick it out during difficult times. Women who crave drama and are up to an emotional roller coaster ride are also likely to hold on tight in a narcissistic relationship. This often means women with a personality disorder, such as Borderline Personality Disorder or Histrionic Personality Disorder. Interestingly, a woman's biology can also influence her choice to maintain a relationship with a narcissist. A study of 237 women found that women are more likely to be attracted to narcissistic traits while ovulating.[74] Because narcissistic men want to date highly attractive women, such women become more likely to become involved with a narcissist. Attractive women can intimidate men without meaning to. Narcissists are assertive and go for what they want, a trait many attractive women find appealing.

What Do You do if You're in Love with a Narcissist?

In the Bible, 2 Timothy verses 3-6 warns:

> Men shall be lovers of self, lovers of money, boastful, haughty, railers, disobedient to parents, unthankful, unholy, without natural affection, implacable, slanderers, without self-control, fierce, no lovers of good, traitors, headstrong, puffed up, lovers of pleasure rather than lovers of God; holding a form of godliness, but having denied the power therefore. From these also turn away. For of these are they that creep into houses, and take captive silly women.

God may be warning you to turn away, but in reality, loving a narcissist is complicated. So, what do you do when you're in love with a narcissist? Most narcissistic traits are not apparent until later in a relationship. I think when we read stories about narcissistic relationships, it is easy to point out where the partner should have left or think of what could have been done differently. The truth is that if narcissists were easy to identify, they would be easy to avoid. As Carrie explained, leaving doesn't solve all problems. Most narcissists put energy into controlling their spouse and leaving isn't easy. Still, most research has concluded that narcissists are incapable of maintaining an equal, give-and-take relationship. Narcissists also have a very difficult time with true intimacy. Does anyone really deserve that?

You've probably heard that the first step to solving a problem is to admit that a problem exists. Although wise, this adage goes against the core nature of narcissism. Narcissists tend to blame others when they face problems. If you are in love with a narcissist and in too deep to make a clean break, seek relationship counseling immediately. A good therapist experienced with NPD can help the narcissist better understand the behaviors that can make relationships intolerable. The other most important thing the partner of a narcissist can do is to develop and enforce clear boundaries. Because of a narcissist's inability to understand the feelings of others, it is important that the partner clearly objectifies boundaries, desires and expectations. For example, "I don't like when you stay out late" is different than "I don't like when you stay out past three in the morning." When an expectation is unclear, the narcissist has an opportunity to exploit it.

Chapter 8

NARCISSISM IN FAMILIES

"All happy families are alike; each unhappy family is unhappy in its own way."

– Leo Tolstoy, *Anna Karenina*

"All parents damage their children. It cannot be helped. Youth, like pristine glass, absorbs the prints of its handlers. Some parents smudge, others crack, a few shatter childhoods completely into jagged little pieces, beyond repair."

– Mitch Albom, *The Five People You Meet in Heaven*

Paul had a pretty good life. At 16, he was a high school football player and enjoyed showing off the vintage mustang his parents bought him for his birthday. He lived in an affluent neighborhood in San Diego, CA with his parents and younger brother. His father was an attorney and his mother was a pre-school teacher. Paul had close friends, was involved in church and had a really cool girlfriend. He was thinking about college and preparing for the SATs. Everything was going so well for Paul that he thought he was in the middle of a nightmare when his father led two uniformed police officers into the backyard where Paul and his brother were swimming in the family's swimming pool. Dressed only in swim shorts, Paul was taken away in handcuffs.

After Paul's parents bailed him out of jail, he learned the reason for his arrest. His father had a sex addiction. He had placed hidden cameras in rental apartments that the family owned. Paul's father was unwilling to take responsibility for his behavior and pointed the finger at his teenage son. The police, and eventually a judge, had no problem believing that a teenage boy, who often helped with minor maintenance duties around the apartment complex, was behind the lewd peeping. Paul's father figured that because he was an attorney, and because Paul was a minor, no permanent harm would be done. Free of criminal charges, Paul's father settled with his victims, who were low-income immigrants, happy to receive money and avoid any legal process. Paul's mother had no knowledge of the sex addiction and was caught between a desire to protect her son and a need to protect her family's image. During family therapy it became clear that Paul's father had NPD. His disorder had poisoned the entire family's dynamic.

Overview of the Narcissistic Parent

Just like with any person, there are individual differences among narcissistic parents. Narcissistic traits tread many gray areas, and there is no single way to raise children through a narcissistic lens. Still, there are some characteristics shared by most narcissistic parents. Most notably, narcissistic parents see their children as extensions of themselves. This often means that they become angry or critical as their children develop into individuals with their own thoughts and ideas. Interestingly, the narcissistic parent can still be extremely loving and giving. Both narcissistic mothers and fathers will invest a great deal of time and energy helping their child develop intellectually, artistically, and in athletics. Having a high-achieving child is to the narcissist, a signal of a job well done. The narcissistic parent will also work really hard to look like a perfect parent. In mothers, this often displays as being "super mom." The narcissistic mother will have clean, well-groomed children, an immaculate home, and be involved in her children's school and activities. Narcissistic parents are often very judgmental. They may not want their children to go to public school or play with certain children because they feel superior. A narcissistic parent may abruptly pull their child from school other activities for perceived injustices.

A narcissistic parent will make judgments about the way others raise their children, often focusing on unimportant details, such as minor uncleanliness. For example, one woman I worked with, who spent several hours a week preparing her daughter for beauty pageants, didn't want her children to play with the little girl across the street because she "ran around without shoes." This penchant for seeing things a specific way and judging others who don't comply can be manifested as racial or religious intolerance. As a result of many of these traits, adult children of narcissists tend to be perfectionists and are often very well organized, physically attractive and protective parents.

The Religious Narcissistic Parent

It is not uncommon for narcissistic parents to be very religious. Many narcissistic people find a sense of belonging in religion, and religious involvement provides a sense of being "right." Evangelical Christianity provides support to the narcissistic parents. Popular Christian parenting books, such as *To Train up a Child* by Michael and Debi Pearl, and *Dare to Discipline* by Dr. James Dobson explains that children are willfully defiant and must learn to respect authority from a very young age. Children who disobey should be spanked immediately. These Christian parenting models depict the parent-child relationship as a battle of wills that the parent must win at all costs. This approach is extremely convenient for the narcissistic parent who operates that way in most relationships. "I'm the parent, you're the child" means to the narcissist "I'm right, you're wrong, I'm powerful, you are not, I'm important, you're not." More importantly, the religious narcissistic parent can hide behind these parenting books when things go wrong, as they inevitably do in authoritarian parenting styles. When the child or anyone else suggests a parenting style based on mutual respect, the narcissist has an entire community of support.

The High Achieving Narcissistic Parent

The high achieving narcissistic mother is likely to volunteer in the classroom, chair the school's parent organization, plan great birthday parties, coach soccer and teach Sunday school. In these cases, the narcissistic mother does not need to brag about her accomplishments because others can see them. Another reason that narcissistic mothers, like narcissists in general, tend to over-extend themselves is because they don't think that others can do as good a job as they can.

Thanks to gender role expectations, keeping up appearances is often easier for narcissistic fathers. A narcissistic father can fulfill his duties simply by financially supporting his family, and anything more is a bonus. In families where the parents are not together, paying child support is often enough, and the narcissistic father will remind everyone that he pays. The high achieving narcissistic parents often respond to their child's burgeoning independence by becoming over-protective. These parents resist letting their children play outside alone or take risks in physical play, even when developmentally appropriate.

Another strategy used by the high achieving narcissistic parent is to make self-deprecating comments in the hopes others will disagree. "I am a terrible mother!" or "I should have been there more when you were growing up" are common, but are not meant as apologies. A more subtle way that over-achieving narcissistic parents will seek affirmation is from comments such as "I'm so tired!" or complaints about children that aren't true or very serious. These comments will often receive a response praising the parent's hard work and effort. The narcissistic parent is unlikely to address the emotional deficits of the child. Because narcissists tend to experience very shallow emotions, criticism is typically met with anger, and rarely an apology or effort to make changes.

For the high achieving parent—whether narcissistic or not, parenthood can become exhausting. Donna and Keith were looking for help managing their teenage son. They had three boys, but were having particular difficulty with their sixteen-year-old, Austin. Their complaints were relatively standard for first-time parents of a teenager. They were concerned about the music Austin listened to, the video games he played, how late he slept on weekends, his friends, his clothes, and his grades. They had also caught him ditching mass more than once, and they were concerned because Austin's girlfriend did not share the family's faith. Donna explained that they had "done everything" and nothing seemed to work. Very often in family therapy, particularly with troubled children, when parents say they have "done everything" they really have done nothing but expect their children to change. I was interested to hear Donna's long list of interventions. To make sure that Austin's music was appropriate for the family's values, he was required to turn in his iPod every Monday so his parents could inspect it for any songs with bad words or sexual content. They had strict rules for video games, and all computers and game systems were in public areas of the house. To monitor his grades, Donna had coordinated a daily progress report system with each of Austin's seven teachers so that every afternoon, she knew what his current grades were and what homework assignments were due. To prevent Austin from sleeping in, he had weekend chores that must be completed before he could do anything else, and they typically woke him up at 8:00 a.m. To prevent Austin from leaving mass, he was forced to sit with his parents instead of attending the church's teen service.

Just hearing about Donna and Keith's efforts to keep their son in line made me feel stressed and tired. And while there is nothing wrong with parental limits, and being aware of a child's activities, I wondered *how could they have the energy for this? When so many parents' problems stem from being unaware, where do they find the energy to be involved in every aspect of Austin's life?* As confusing as this was initially, the answer was clear: Donna and Keith saw Austin as an extension of themselves, not as a young man developing into a person with unique thoughts, beliefs and values. Many of their measures were consistent with keeping their child safe. For example, keeping computers, televisions and gaming systems in public areas of the home in a common tactic recommended by experts for media safety. When Donna discussed areas in which she was unsuccessful in managing Austin, such as his choice of girlfriends or the way he dressed, she said more than once that he was a reflection of her. She also expressed feelings of embarrassment over Austin's behavior. To some degree, children are a reflection of their parents, but as they get older, this becomes less. During adolescence, children become more influenced by their peers, teachers, hobbies and other interests. I don't believe that Donna and Keith are clinically narcissistic, but their inability to see their son as a separate person is indicative of a narcissistic trait that allowed them to take his independence as a threat while damaging their relationship with their son and disrupting the peace in their home.

The Pushy Narcissistic Parent

Plenty of non-narcissistic parents raise accomplished children who excel in academics or extracurricular activities. An important distinction is that the pushy narcissistic parent pushes their children into activities that the child doesn't enjoy in order to fulfill their own emotional needs. A relevant example can be found at any child beauty pageant. It's possible that some little girls may enjoy spray tans, false eyelashes, extreme makeup and adult clothing and dance moves. However, from a developmental perspective, most children prefer to play without pressure or competition. Reality television programs that showcase pageant children regularly feature competitive, angry parents who clearly aren't there for their child's benefit.

Even with a distinction between narcissistic and non-narcissistic traits, gray areas remain. Richard Williams is famous for being the father and coach of tennis stars Serena and Venus Williams. Combined, the sisters' trophy case includes nine Olympic gold medals in addition to dozens of other championships. Sure, Williams has pushed his daughters to be among the best female athletes in the world, but his approach has clearly kept his children's interest before his own. In spite of their success, he has encouraged his daughters to focus on education and enjoy their own hobbies and interests outside of tennis. He has also relied on community during tough times. In 2000, he told *Ebony* magazine, "I had black people- my people- who were so high on what we were doing. Every time I was criticized by those people who thought I was doing things the wrong way, there were blacks who told me I was doing it the right way."[79]

In 2009, Williams discussed parenting with journalist John Intini. Williams is a pushy parent, and he claims he has known his girls would be champions since preschool, but also expressed an earnest desire for happy, well-balanced children. "A child [needs to understand] real life. Parents protect their kids so when a kid grows up and leaves home that child thinks everything is nice, that child thinks everyone is truthful, that child thinks everything is great. But life is not that way. I'd take them to the police department where they could see people in jail. I wanted them to see people on drugs. I wanted them to see how athletes make some of the worst decisions and lose their money at an early age. If you can see it from the beginning then you can learn."[80]

Williams was also aware of the danger of pushing kids too hard. "If your child is going to be super good and the child has confidence, your child can be great. But when you push the child too much, you don't give the child confidence. The reason I took Venus and Serena out of tennis [in 1991] is because I saw kids from the best neighborhoods, like Beverly Hills, with broken wrists. I've seen kids get pushed and damaged. You see kids that are told they're nothing. That's past the extreme."[80] And finally, when asked the most important thing he has taught his daughters, Williams replied "How to love God. How to love themselves. It's a dangerous thing when a woman loves herself, because she has confidence. Most men do not like a woman who has confidence. They're scared of her. If a woman is taught to love God, to love herself, and you implant confidence, you cannot tear her down. That's why Serena and Venus were so good."[80]

However, in the same interview, Williams expressed an inflated sense of self. When asked why he now makes fewer headlines than in years past, he responded, "I don't make as many headlines because I've asked parts of the media not to film me no more and I won't do interviews no more. But I don't know no one who wouldn't want to interview me. When I get ready to go speak with Obama, that will easily be done. I'm Richard Williams. And Richard Williams can do anything he wants to. When I'm in England, if I want to go see the Queen, I can do that. I just don't want it no more."[80] Nobody outside the Williams family can truly know if Richard Williams is motivated by narcissistic traits or a true desire to do the best for his now adult daughters. However, he is a clear example of the gray area between loving parent and self-loving narcissist.

The Conniving Narcissistic Parent

Narcissistic parents can often be conniving. According to Nina Brown, author of *Children of the Self-Absorbed*, "This parent will lie, cheat, distort, and mislead in order to achieve her goals. Others, including her children, are considered fair game for manipulation and exploitation. She can be adept at reading other's needs and emotional susceptibility and using these to manipulate and exploit them."[81] Shanna Harper was 13 years old when her mother was arrested in 1991. She was practicing her cheerleading routine in the garage her mother customized with mirrors and a dance floor. Her mother, Texas housewife and church organist Wanda Holloway, calmly placed her jewelry on the kitchen counter and left compliantly with the officers. After posting a $10,000 bail the next day, Holloway returned to her suburban home to explain the horrible situation she had created for her entire family and community.[82]

Holloway had been arrested for plotting to kill Verna Heath, the mother of a cheerleader that Holloway perceived as a rival of Shanna's. Initially, Holloway offered her former brother-in-law $7,500 to kill Heath and her 13-year-old daughter, Amber. Later, she decided that Amber would be overcome by grief at losing her mother and likely drop out of cheer all together. She offered $2,500 for Heath's murder. Holloway assumed that her brother-in-law would agree to the murder because he was a convicted felon. Instead, he recorded several exchanges between himself and Holloway and turned the recordings over to police. During one recording, she handed over a pair of earrings valued at $2,500, intended as a down payment.[82]

Wanda's obsession with Shanna's cheerleading success started when Shanna was only five and intensified as she got older. Although Shanna and Amber had been friends, competition eventually drove them apart. When both girls were both up for a coveted spot on the school cheer team, Wanda made her daughter pass out personalized pencils and rulers. Campaigning was against school rules and Shanna was disqualified. The position was given to Amber.

Like many narcissists, Wanda had experienced several failed marriages. At the time of the murder plot, she was married to the owner of a pipeline-construction company. She bragged to friends—and anyone who would listen—that she was worth more than $2 million, could buy as much jewelry as she wanted, and that she kept large amounts of cash around the house. Having a successful cheerleader daughter was a step in Wanda's path to being a socialite in her town. Shanna didn't particularly enjoy cheer, but she was forced through intense practices, even when injured. Amber's success in cheer was a threat to Wanda's identity and the identity she had constructed for her child. Additionally, because Wanda viewed Shanna as an extension of herself, she assumed that Amber was naturally an extension of Verna. In one of the recorded exchanges between Wanda and her hopeful hit man, she explained that she was very concerned that Shanna would not make the cheer team in her final year of junior high school. "This is a critical year. She don't make it this year, she ain't never gonna make it." Her brother-in-law pointed out that it would be difficult kill a child and she replied, "But, Terry, you don't know this little girl," she snapped. "If you knew her—ooh! I can't stand her. I mean, she's a bitch. Makes me sick. I mean, I could knock her in the face, you know?" The day after Wanda handed her earrings over to her brother-in-law, she was arrested. It took less than a year for her to be convicted of solicitation of murder.[83]

While on bail awaiting appeal, Wanda told reporters, "I never have tried to live through my child. We are so close; we even wear a lot of the same clothes. A lot of hers are too trendy for me, but I wear them anyway."[83] Although Holloway was sentenced to fifteen years in prison, she only served six months. While many feel that six months was not long enough, Holloway's bizarre narcissistic behaviors were enough to damage her daughter for life. Immediately after the arrest, Shanna began experiencing debilitating depression and anxiety attacks. She was ostracized at school, where students and teachers knew what her mother had done. Two made for TV movies were made about the incident, and before long, the entire country knew Shanna's name. Actress Holly Hunter won an Emmy for her portrayal of Wanda.

Eventually, with the help of therapy, Shanna was able to get past the injuries caused by her mother. Today, she is a married teacher and mother of two boys. Although she maintains contact with her mother, she told people magazine, "We don't have mother-daughter talks, but she's very helpful, and we talk about the boys all the time."[84] The story of Wanda Holloway is an extreme one. Still, there is no doubt that she displayed signs of narcissism long before she resorted to plotting murder. Holloway believed she was deserving of a certain status, and was willing to do whatever it took to achieve that status. She bragged about her material worth, and saw her child as an extension of herself. Ultimately, Wanda saw her adversaries as disposable objects, not people. Her own self-interest—that is, her daughter's success in cheerleading, was more valuable than Verna Heath being alive to raise her four children.

The Emotionally Needy Narcissistic Parent

A tendency to depend on their children to meet their emotional needs rather than working to meet the child's emotional needs is common among narcissistic parents. This is a common theme among alcoholic families, but is also seen in families fraught with narcissism. Depending on the individual's emotional maturity, this can take many forms. For some parents, this may mean sharing personal details of their marriage with their children. For other parents, this means taking a child's failures personally, such as becoming angry when a child forgets a line in a play or performs poorly during a soccer game. They may ask a toddler "do you love me?" or make a statement such as "you're my best friend," "I love you when you perform ballet" or "If you love me, you will practice your guitar." Care-taking children are also the most likely to be under the control of their parents into adulthood because they did not have healthy opportunities to exercise autonomy during childhood. Care-taking children experience an array of difficulties during adulthood, including a desire to please others, even when they feel they are being manipulated. After being told that their behavior makes a parent feel a certain way for their entire lives, as adults, they often find themselves in difficult situations because of feeling as though they need to meet the emotional needs of others.

The Emotionally Controlling Narcissistic Parent

The emotionally controlling narcissistic parent is similar to the emotionally needy parent, because he or she often expects the child to take on adult responsibilities. At the same time, this parent uses his or child's emotional needs for personal gain.

Sara described her mother, Robin as a "super mom who raised four kids, made dinners, and was involved in baseball." However, she often had emotional breakdowns and holding a knife, once threatened to "end it all" in front of her husband and children. She often had angry outbursts of yelling, slamming doors, and breaking things. Around the time Sara started high school, Robin started a part-time job and became emotionally distant. Sara's father asked her to clean the house and complete other household chores before Robin got home each day.

One day, Robin asked Sara if she had a friend she could spend the day with. When she asked why, her mother told her she was going somewhere for the day, but didn't want her husband to find out, so instead she would tell him she was spending the day with Sara. She promised to make it up with a *real* outing soon. Sara remembers being very excited because Robin hadn't tried to bond with her in years. This went on for months, but Robin never made good on her promise to take Sara out for a mother-daughter day. Not long after, Robin began taking computer classes on nights and weekends. Sara's father was suspicious and asked Sara and a friend to follow her. They drove for over an hour and ended up in a resort town where Robin was meeting a man. When Sara confronted her mom, Robin threatened to tell Sara's dad that Sara had helped her sneak around if she said a word. Sara stayed quiet for months, became depressed and spent less time with friends. One night, when her mother left for "computer class," Sara told her dad everything. Robin became so enraged, she punched Sara in the face, pulled her hair, and demanded that she tell her father she was lying for attention. She refused, and her father moved out of the house a few days later. She remembers that neither parent would speak to her. She thinks that her dad still blames her today.

Sara became pregnant when she was 16. She was legally emancipated from both parents, got married and moved to another state. She didn't hear from her parents for several years. One day, Sara's sister called and said Robin was *suffering* without Sara and the kids in her life, and would do anything to be a family again. Sara was reluctant at first, but her relationship with Robin seemed to go better this time around. Sara was having trouble in her own marriage, and as Sara put it, "Robin was quick to play the hero." Sara and her three small children left the state and moved in with Robin and her new husband. "They wanted me to look for a job and work, so that's what I did. I found a dream job as a counter manager for a cosmetics line," explained Sara. On the day Sara was supposed to start her new job, her mother refused to baby-sit. Robin screamed at Sara and called her names in front of her children. Robin involved Sara's sister, and before long, the fight was physical. Robin told Sara to leave and not come back. Within minutes, she was on the streets with three small children, including an infant. They hitched a ride into town, and Sara called her estranged husband to pick them up. This pattern continued. Robin would call Sara about something serious in the family (one time, Sara's grandfather had cancer, another time, Robin heard from a family member that Sara was having serious health issues and was recovering from surgery). These interactions opened the doors of communication, and both times, Sara took her mother's offer to leave her husband and move back home. Each time, Sara and her children have been kicked out of the house within a few months, always following a dramatic and often violent fight. Today, Sara does not have a relationship with either parent, although all three of her siblings have a relationship with both parents.

You can see from this story that Robin emotionally manipulated Sara for her own needs. When Sara was young, Robin expected her to lie for her, and when she didn't, Robin became enraged. For whatever reason, Robin would contact Sara every few years to "make peace" (notice she never apologized) and the moment the arrangement was no longer beneficial to her, she cut ties swiftly and without notice. From an outsider's perspective, it may be easy to lay some of the later blame on Sara. *After all, she should know better.* An emotionally manipulative narcissist understands the weaknesses of others, and this case, Sara was desperate for a loving and close relationship with her mother.

Challenges Faced by Children of Narcissists

Charlotte is the adult daughter of a narcissist. She has struggled to forgive her father for most of her life, and decided more than two years ago to completely cut off communication. Recently, Charlotte's father has been calling her cell phone several times a week. When he was tired of her ignoring his calls, he used the Internet to find her work number. When she hung up on him abruptly, he called her mother, from whom he has been divorced for over a decade, and cried about the disintegration of his relationship with his daughter. When I asked Charlotte about the contents of the voice mail messages her father leaves, she told me that he usually says he doesn't know why she is mad at him. He has never apologized for the physical, verbal and emotional abuse or for using drugs in the family home. As frustrating and hurtful as Charlotte's experience is, it is entirely possible that her father doesn't know what he did wrong. Narcissistic parents measure their success by external events. Charlotte's father never had any problem keeping up appearances. Nobody in the community, including Charlotte's best friend knew what was going on behind closed doors. He held down a job, supported his family, and made sure the children drank a glass of milk with every meal. The family attended church every Sunday, and he was there to attend softball games, school plays, and to scream at teachers for poor test scores and late homework assignments. In her father's mind, the bad things, the emotional situations are inconsequential. After all, it doesn't count if others can't see and admire it.

Charlotte's story is a clear illustration of the shallow emotions experienced by narcissists, and the empty apologies that result when they feel backed into a corner. A parent with NPD will typically ignore or be unaware of his or her child's boundaries. In general, narcissists avoid direct apologies. Like in Charlotte's experience, the narcissistic parent cannot take criticism from his or her own children. The child of a narcissist can, from an early age sense a lack of emotional connection from his parent. Both childhood complaints ("You never play with me!") and adult complaints ("You pushed me too hard as a child!") are met with a laundry list of defenses. *I sent you to the best school...It's not my fault your mother blew the child support money... you had everything you ever wanted...I sacrificed so much for you, you are so ungrateful...* "Without therapeutic intervention, narcissistic parents are unlikely to ever take full responsibility for the hurt they have caused.

Most of the time, the generational effects of narcissism are more subtle. For example, Teresa is a mother of three adult children who recognizes narcissistic traits in herself, her mother, and one of her children. She explained, "My Mom sustained a major head injury at age 18, and it left her an epileptic. This in itself can affect personality, as can the drugs, especially long term. So, she exhibits narcissistic tendencies to some degree. She is not a caregiver. My dad told me he would come home from work when I was a baby and often find me in need of care. She did pretty good taking care of my physical needs when I was older, but was pretty absent emotionally. Interaction was always on her terms, not mine, unless I was sick or something.

"I've been full of fear since I was little, of everything and everyone. This has lessened over time. I never felt *good enough* at anything. That's still an issue. I've also recognized a lot of selfishness and a lack of empathy in myself. I started noticing it years ago. For example, I can't stand to see someone vomit. That meant when one of my kids was sick, I'd either hold them over the sink, or leave the room until they were done. I've seen other women put their hands under a baby's mouth as it was vomiting to catch it, and it didn't bother them a bit. They were more focused on the baby's needs than their own. I still fight these tendencies every day. I'm usually late to everything, and for years saw it only from my point of view, and not of the person waiting for me. My husband often comes home after work with the same basic worries and concerns every day, and it's hard to be empathetic. Not that I need it to be all about me anymore, but I often brush it off or minimize it or get impatient hearing the same things over and over. And I fight a judgmental and *know it all* streak, too. Being *right* about everything was really important to me for a long time."

Compliance, Rebellion and Confusion

Some children of narcissists respond with rebellion. They realize that pleasing the parent is impossible and give up early. During the teen and adult years, these children act as though they don't care what others think and effectively ignore the feelings of others. These children often seem insensitive, or seem as though they want to debate or pick fights. These adults have a difficult time with stress and often struggle to build meaningful relationships.[81] The adult child of a narcissist has another unique problem. He or she often experiences depression and anxiety as an adult without knowing why. Because narcissistic parents are experts at making everything look good, the child of the narcissist may not know anything was wrong. A common response in therapy is "I had a great childhood with caring parents. I *should* be happy." These adult children often feel inadequate, as though they *should* have accomplished more. "My mother was married with kids by the time she was my age, and I don't even have a boyfriend" or "My father had a successful career and I can't even finish college." Similarly, an adult going through this emotional crisis may feel ungrateful, selfish, dramatic or needy for not appreciating his or her parents.[85] Consider Shanna Harper. Had her mother not plotted to kill an innocent woman, Shanna may have never understood the toxicity in her family. She may have grown up believing, like the rest of her community, that she had a wonderful childhood. After all, she was her mother's top priority throughout her entire childhood. In interviews, Shanna described her relationship with her mother as very close and expressed a desire to please her.[84]

Children of narcissists also face confusion because their siblings often experienced childhood differently. Narcissists often choose one child to favor, or one child to reject, sometimes both. When a narcissistic couple raises their children together, each may pick a different target, or the same.[85] During Wanda Holloway's murder trial, which received heavy media attention, very little was known about her older son, Shanna's brother. No evidence suggests that he was abused or loathed by Holloway, but he certainly didn't receive the constant coaching and attention that Wanda showered over Shanna. Favoring one child over another can create tension among siblings. The favored sibling may view the less favored sibling in a negative light, believing him or her to have been lazy, argumentative, or unappreciative. It is unlikely that either sibling will understand that the parents, not the children created these identities.

To further confuse matters, many unknowing friends and members of the community are envious of the narcissistic family. *Your mom is so beautiful. I wish my home as clean as Cindy's. I can't even get my dad to come to my soccer games, your dad has coached every season since kindergarten. Can I eat dinner at your house? Your mom is a great cook.* These experiences often compound the guilty feelings experienced by the children of narcissists. How can everything really be so wrong when everyone else thinks it is so right?

Gender Roles within the Narcissistic Family

You may have noticed at this point, that almost all of the families and couples discussed in this book tend to adhere to traditional gender roles. We've talked about stay-at-home moms who bake apple pies and fathers who work hard and coach sports teams. Little research has been done to investigate the relationship between narcissism and gender role, except that original Freudian theory saw it as an extension of male homosexuality. In Dr. Pinsky's study examining celebrity and narcissism, he found that in all sub groups of celebrities he examined (actors, comedians, reality stars and musicians), women had higher levels of narcissistic traits than their male colleagues. Pinsky inferred that the pressure on women in entertainment to be attractive and sexually desirable is an important factor in this finding.[86]

What I have found from my clinical research and interviews with narcissistic families, narcissistic parents almost always adhere to traditional gender roles, even when narcissists in general do not. Another common finding is that narcissistic men tend to marry women in gender-traditional careers such as teachers and nurses. A possible reason is that men with fragile egos assume that women in traditional female careers are not intimidating and may be more compliant. Narcissistic mothers thrive as homemakers. Sufficient research does not exist to understand exactly why this is. One possibility is that by sticking to traditional roles, the narcissistic parent feels further validated by their community and society in general. Social rebels rarely get positive recognition, but those who conform and excel in their roles, tend to get noticed.

Divorce and Parental Disengagement in the Narcissistic Family

Lori was a single mother who, for financial reasons, moved across the state after she divorced Andrew. Their 7-year-old son, Peter was heartbroken and had a difficult time adjusting after the divorce. Andrew had displayed narcissistic traits throughout the marriage, but he was a dedicated and involved father, so Lori expected that he would maintain contact with their son. Andrew's contact with Peter was sporadic and confusing. He frequently changed his phone number without notifying Peter or Lori. He owned an RV and would come to town and spend weeks of quality time with his son. Then, without any notice at all, he would leave. Peter, unable to get a hold of his father, was extremely wounded by these behaviors. It seems that any reasonable person would know that these actions would hurt a child, but Andrew, like many narcissistic fathers, was oblivious.

As discussed in the previous chapter, narcissistic marriages often end in divorce. Divorce in any family can create problems and adjustments for children. Traditionally, mothers tend to get custody of children after a divorce. Still non-custodial fathers play a vital role in the adjustment of their children after a divorce by participating in their lives and by continuing to express love and serve as a male role model. Unfortunately, many fathers do not maintain a relationship with their children following divorce. Approximately 35% of relationships between children and their non-custodial fathers are disrupted after a divorce.[87] Reasons range from geography and financial constraints to contention and litigation between parents.

Divorce is particularly difficult for the narcissistic father, because during marriage, simply being in the house and going about his daily routine fulfilled the majority of fatherly duties. After a divorce, the narcissistic father may keep up appearances by fighting for custody. Custody requests are often unreasonable, and when they don't work out, the child or mother is blamed. Narcissism impairs range of emotion, and the narcissistic father often can't understand or consider what his children are feeling.

The narcissistic father's distortion of reality and exaggeration of self create a confusing situation for his family. Their words *"I want full custody," "The kids are better off living with me"* contradict their actions. These men do not take responsibility for the disintegrating relationship with their children, but instead blame their spouse, the courts, or the children. These fathers do not see themselves as abandoning their children, but instead see themselves as victims who have been abandoned. Interestingly, the most disengaged fathers are the ones who report missing their children the most, thinking of them the most and feeling the most hurt over the changes in their relationship. Mediation is often unsuccessful in these cases because the narcissistic father expects the mediator to take his side and feels attacked by the system when things don't go according to his wishes.

Parental Alienation in the Narcissistic Family

Parental alienation is another problem common the narcissistic family. Unlike the parent who detaches, a parental alienator (PA) develops a close bond with the child as a means of undermining the other parent's relationship with the child. Parental alienation can occur to some degree in any relationship involving children, but it tends to be more severe when one parent has narcissistic traits. In severe cases of parental alienation, the PA aims to cut all ties between the child and other parent by limiting access.[88] PAs tend to be mothers, but this is usually attributed to traditional custody arrangements, not gender specific traits. Any parent who has more custody than the other can become a PA.

Parental alienation has a profound effect on children. They often experience depression, which can lead to suicide, and behavioral problems such as lying, stealing, substance abuse and violence. Tracey, a young woman whose parents divorced when she was four years old explained, "My dad allegedly falsified court documents with his new girlfriend causing my mother to miss her actual court appearance and gained full custody of my sister and I. I will never forget the day we moved with my dad and we were in our moving truck. Looking outside of the glass and waving bye to my mommy. I was so sad, I knew then that things would never be the same. From then on my dad held my sister and I as bait in order to get my mom back. He called us a *package deal*. For years he hid us and my mom had no idea where we were or if we were OK." Tracey experienced hurt growing up, beyond being separated from her mother. Her father did not have the financial resources to care for his family, and then spent years living with other relatives. Tracey consistently felt like an outsider and yearned for a family to which she could belong.

The process of parental alienation itself can create narcissistic traits in the child. The child grows up seeing problems blamed on one parent by the PA, and becomes arrogant and entitled, with few skills for solving problems besides blaming others. Although parental alienation syndrome has not yet been adopted by any edition of the DSM, the term is often used to describe the psychological and behavioral symptoms children experience when being raised by a PA. Common symptoms of parental alienation include a strong hatred for one parent; beliefs that strongly align with those of the PA and being unable to support thoughts and ideas about the parent with personal experience, but instead with information learned from the other parent. This can be very confusing, because when a child loses a parent to detachment, these behaviors and feelings are relatively normal. Statements such as "*My dad was never there for me*" or "*My mom was a drug addict*" may seem appropriate in a single parent home. However, a distinction between parental detachment and parental alienation is the child of a PA has a passionate hatred toward the other parent. In many cases, the child's hatred extends to other family members or friends who support the alienated parent. The child also views himself as an ally of the PA and they are often up against the world.

Parental Alienation and the Pseudo-mature Child

Just as many children raised by PAs develop a sense of entitlement, many develop pseudo-maturity, or patterns of behaving much older than their actual age. The pseudo-mature child is one who seems to have passed over childhood completely and behaves in many ways as an adult. Pseudo-maturity occurs when the child tries (unconsciously in most cases) to behave more competently than she really is in order to meet the emotional needs of the parent. Pseudo-maturity develops in response to a variety of childhood traumas in addition to[89] parental alienation. It is often over-looked during childhood because the parent and others see it as a positive attribute. The goal as a parent is to raise a mature adult, and when those behaviors are displayed early, it somehow feels like an accomplishment. Pseudo-maturity is a problem in itself because the social maturity is not matched with equal emotional or psychological maturity. During early childhood, social maturity may not seem like a problem, but during adolescence, it often leads to early sexual activity and drug or alcohol abuse. The pseudo-mature child is also more likely than her peers to dye hair, pierce body parts and get tattoos than her peers.[89] These "mature" behaviors lead to even more trouble as the child creates relationships with older adolescents and young adults. It is developmentally appropriate for a 20-year-old man to enjoy a sexual relationship, but a 15-year-old girl, no matter how "mature," is not an appropriate partner.

Narcissistic Children

In Chapter 1, we discussed several characteristics of childhood narcissism. Overall, most experts believe that narcissism originates from one of two childhood circumstances. The first perspective is that the child is over-indulged and spoiled, and then believes that he or she is special and more deserving than others. The other perspective is that the child uses an over-inflated sense of self to compensate for painful feelings related to hurt, abuse or trauma.

The Permissive Childhood

Some parents fail to discipline their children for fear of rejection or confrontation. Other parents feel guilty for circumstances they perceive to be out of their control. They feel as though they must be permissive or indulgent because the child has poor self-esteem, one parent is absent, because they work and aren't home as much as they would like, or any of a cornucopia of reasons. Non-custodial parents are reluctant to discipline because they want the small amount of time they spend with their children to be fun. Oftentimes, parents minimize the degree to which their children call the shots, or make up excuses. One mother, who had just bought her 12-year-old daughter an expensive Smart phone for the third time after the previous phones had been lost or broken, explained that she keeps buying them because, "She will just nag until she gets one." This results in a child who feels above the law and sees others as objects that can be manipulated. Because these children routinely violate their parents' boundaries, they are never taught to respect or even identify boundaries. It is not news that spoiling a child has catastrophic consequences. Proverbs 13:24 warned us, "He that spareth his rod hateth his son, but he that loveth him chasteneth him betimes." In 1377, William Langland wrote, "Who-so spareth ye srynge, spilleth his children." For centuries now, we have known that sparing the rod spoils a child. The proverbial rod has many definitions, ranging from a literal rod, to any set of consequences for bad behavior. Any way it is defined, children need love, discipline and boundaries to grow into healthy adults.

The Traumatic Childhood

The second perspective sees narcissism as a defense mechanism for hurt or trauma. An inflated sense of self allows these children to feel adequate at worst and superior at best. In many of these cases, the children are at some point, left to teach themselves skills needed to become a socially and emotionally functioning adult. When children must care for themselves, or others before they are developmentally ready, their sense of self-worth becomes dependent on an ability to perform. When they are unable to do something correctly, they feel a great sense of shame. The rest of their sense of self becomes a struggle to avoid shame, humiliation and feelings of failure.

Overview of the Narcissistic Child

It is possible for the experiences of indulgence and trauma to overlap. Adopted children, for example, may have a traumatic beginning and later have parents who derive great pleasure from their presence and praise everything they do. Children from divorced families can also experience a traumatic hurt and then be indulged by either or both parents. Lance, whose narcissistic behaviors were described in Chapter 1, had a combination of over-indulgence and a need to repair feelings of hurt. His mother came to his rescue whenever he faced consequences at school. At the same time, she was a single mother who worked long hours. Lance's father had left after a contentious divorce and he was unable to contact him.

No matter the reason for a child's narcissism, the narcissistic child runs the household. These children have a difficult time making and maintaining friendships. They may seem negative and prone to arguments. When trapped, they are extremely dramatic and self-deprecating. Narcissistic children are master manipulators. They know exactly what it takes to get what they want from their parents and other adults in their lives. Whether it is faking nice, screaming for hours on end, or pulling their own hair, the narcissistic child always wins. Narcissistic children grow up, and the dynamics change. For many people, overt narcissistic traits are not apparent until adulthood. No matter when narcissism begins in an individual, the entire family is poisoned.

Stephanie was a hard working single mom. Her daughter Emily had struggled a little when Stephanie was going through cancer treatment, but it did not seem like anything out of the ordinary. Emily was extraordinarily beautiful, and when she was growing up, people would quip, "Watch out for her, you'll have to beat the boys off with a stick." Emily took great pride in her looks. Once at a grocery store, a little girl asked Emily if she was princess. When Emily was 22, she began dating Troy and everything changed. Troy was consistently rude to Stephanie and before long, Emily had little contact with the family. At first, Stephanie and her family were concerned that Emily may be in an abusive relationship. Troy was very unpleasant in public; it seemed likely that he could be aggressive, even violent behind closed doors. But after years passed and relationships became more strained, it was clear that Emily was capable of making her own choices. Emily was extremely abusive toward her mother. She and her boyfriend purchased a home in the same neighborhood, and she routinely drove past the house to curse or throw garbage at the house. She told friends and family members that her mother abused her while she was growing up, which Stephanie vehemently denies. Stephanie fell into a deep depression, not understanding why her daughter would cut ties and be so cruel. In addition to the painful relationship she had with her daughter, Stephanie's breast cancer reappeared and she was responsible for caring for aging parents. During this time, Stephanie's parents began receiving calls from a credit reporting agency warning that their identity had been compromised. Eager to resolve the problem, they gave personal information to the caller. Months later, they learned that the caller was Emily and she used the information to steal several thousands of dollars from her own grandparents. Emily and her boyfriend had been running a scam, targeting the elderly and they ended up leaving the country to evade justice. Seeing her own parents be victimized by Emily was the final straw for Stephanie.

After six years, she was finally able to let go of her hopes for her daughter and begin to mourn the loss, as if she had died.

Narcissism Effects Multiple Generations

Narcissists can inflict toxicity on multiple generations at once. Rosanna is an ICU nurse. She has seen several displays of family dynamics—both healthy and unhealthy, but the behavior of one particular woman perplexed her. She was caring for a 72-year-old man who was not expected to recover after a stroke. Like most ICU patients at the end of life, the man's family was with him every day. Among the family members, his oldest daughter, Pam seemed to stand out. She had a very strong personality, and spoke loudly. Her presence was obvious every time she walked into the department. She began taking measures to manage his care, telling the nurses what to do, and demanding to talk to doctors only minutes after they had consulted with Pam's mother. She often made comments to the nurses about her own medical knowledge. On several occasions, she said "I almost became a doctor" as if letting hospital staff know she was their equal. She told one doctor that she knew the president of the hospital. Pam also became extremely pushy with her own family. As her father's condition progressed, she began to prepare for his death. She criticized her mother for going home at the end of each day instead of spending the night at her husband's bedside. Instead of considering the individual thoughts and feelings of each family member, she demanded that her children, siblings, and other family members all be in the room as he died. Her mother felt that none of the younger children should visit at all, and a battle ensued. Pam's devaluation of her siblings, her own children and other family members was a clear attempt to establish herself as the *best* child. She decided that her way of grieving and handling her father's death was the *right* way.

Narcissism in families creates a unique set of problems because the people (often victims) involved are desperate to love the narcissist in their lives. As humans, we are wired to love our parents, and children. The process of recognizing toxicity in someone we want to love creates feelings of confusion, shame, anger, guilt and sadness. Like addictions and other mental disorders, narcissistic traits create problems for multiple generations. It is important for any person who loves a narcissist (or who is unable to get out from the control of narcissist) to understand that he or she cannot fix the narcissist, and he or she does not need to suffer alone. Isolation is a common experience for many people who have a narcissist in the family. Because the narcissist can so easily please people, outsiders may not understand that something terribly wrong is happening behind closed doors. A family member may not be able to get treatment for a loved one with NPD, but he or she deserves to take the struggle seriously and ask for help.

Chapter 9

NARCISSISM IN THE CHURCH

"A man can no more diminish God's glory by refusing to worship
Him than a lunatic can put out the sun by scribbling the word 'darkness' on
the walls of his cell."

– C.S. Lewis, *The Problem of Pain*

"Sometimes the Bible in the hand of one man is worse than a whisky bottle in
the hand of (another)... There are just some kinds of men who - who're so busy
worrying about the next world they've never learned to live in this one, and
you can look down the street and see the results."

– Harper Lee, *To Kill a Mockingbird*

In a commercial for a reality show called *Preachers of L.A.*, a minister says, "You seen my Bentley, You seen my glory, but you don't know my story." A well-known anti-gay activist and co-founder of a major Christian ministry is caught returning from an expensive European trip with a male prostitute. A minister claims that God will protect him while handling deadly snakes. A cult minister requires young girls to "marry" him in order to be respected members of the church. Nine hundred and twelve people, including infants and small children, die in a mass suicide involving poisoned Kool-Aid. From materialism, to sex, to controlling the lives and deaths of others, narcissism is alive and well in the church.

It seems logical to think that religion provides a healthy solution to narcissism. After all, most major world religions promote empathy—the natural anecdote to narcissism. Additionally, all world religions promote group cooperation, and a sense of sameness as opposed to being special or unique. Individuals are often encouraged to use their unique talents—often called "spiritual gifts" in Christianity, to serve the community. The most devout in all religions vow to live as simply as possible. Buddhist monks, for example, eat only what is offered to them, refrain from eating meat, and make their own robes. They use simple furniture, and ask for nothing, taking only what is offered. Catholic nuns live a similar life, but work in the community, typically in schools and hospitals. Fasting, self-control and giving to the poor are among the Five Pillars of Islam. Devout Hindus practice Dharma, which translates to righteousness. This involves living a virtuous lifestyle, practicing self-control, purity, respect, and thinking of others first. If every world religion is based on a system that should essentially stifle the growth of a self-centered, self-serving world view, how is it taking root?

The Leprosy of the Papacy

Pope Francis is *different* from other popes. As the first ever Latin American Pope, the initial sign that changes were coming occurred the moment he stepped onto the balcony of St. Peter's Basilica after his 2013 selection. Instead of the heavily decorated silk vestment typically worn by the leader of the world's largest Christian Church, he wore a simple white robe. As Pope, he made the decision to continue the simple life he lived as a bishop. At 76-years-old, he travels in a Ford Focus, carries his own luggage and prefers a simple wooden chair over the traditional golden papal chair. What's more, he criticized the church for its "obsession" with political issues such as birth control, gay marriage, and abortion, warning that the church will "fall like a house of cards" without a renewed sense of balance. Pope Francis is also the first Pope to openly recognize the narcissism that often comes with leading a church. In an interview, he warned, "Heads of the Church have often been narcissists, flattered and thrilled by their courtiers. The court is the leprosy of the papacy."[90]

Pope Francis understands that narcissistic individuals are often drawn to the glory and recognition offered in religion. Likewise, a healthy person can get caught up in the admiration and recognition involved in leading a church, especially if the church becomes popular and wealthy. Churches in general are becoming more narcissistic. Christianity in the United States, in particular, tends to focus on the individual, rather than more collectivist religions, such as Buddhism. Phrases such as "personal savior" and "Jesus loves you" emphasize the individual, which can attract a person who longs to feel special. Today, churches are businesses as much as anything else, and numbers matter. Visit any mega-church and you will see that vanity and materialism abound. Today, more than 1,300 churches boast a congregation of more than 2,000. In 1970, only 50 such churches existed. Many of these churches have cafes, book stores, fitness centers, and private schools. The sanctuaries have Jumbotron screens, and state-of-the-art audio and film equipment. Traditional church worship teams have been replaced by rock bands. To attract children, children's ministries often have fancy buildings, professional play structures, video games and even pets inside the classrooms. Most offer candy or other prizes for memorizing Bible verses, or just showing up. In 2007, the average mega-church income was $6.5 million. Although missions, structures and service are paid for with that money (members are often able to access food pantries, financial planning classes, free marriage counseling, services in Spanish, tutoring, and zumba classes) about half goes to the salaries of church workers.[91] These churches do plenty of good—for their members and the community, but individuals today who are seeking spirituality are becoming increasingly attracted to churches who can *do something* for them. Being part of a community and serving a higher power are no longer the priority.

From Feeling Used to Feeling Alone in a Fake Apocalypse: How to Know if You are Following a Narcissist

During the winter of 2010, I began to see interesting billboards and bus advertisements in and around Los Angeles. Some said "Save the date!" Another read "Judgment Day," they all announced that the world would end on May 21, 2011. At first, like many others, I thought these billboards were advertising a new movie. But as the day came closer, the campaigns became more difficult to ignore and it was obvious that someone really believed the world was ending. Around this time, I became fascinated with this movement. It was obviously costly, who could be behind it?

Harold Camping was the minister and evangelical radio owner brazenly predicting the end. In 1992, he published a book entitled *1994?* That predicted the world would end in September of 1994. Although he said he was 99% certain that his careful calculations were correct, the day came and went. After his second prediction in 1995 passed without incident, his doomsday prophecies ended for more than a decade. By 2010, Camping was back with another date, and more complicated math. He explained in his radio program *Open Forum,* "Seven thousand years after 4990 B.C., the year of the flood, is the year 2011 A.D. The math involved is 4990, plus 2011, minus one equals 7,000. The Bible has given us absolute proof that the year 2011 is the end of the world, during the Day of Judgment."

This prediction was different than other predictions, however, because this time, the movement had more money and more followers than ever before. Individual believers paid for billboards and newspaper ads. They left their jobs to pass out tracts and drive cross-country in vans and RVs reminding the country that the end was near. Although isolation was not part of the doctrine, many followers left their spouses and children, and disengaged from friendships because the people in their lives did not understand or agree with their faith. Many more put their children through unneeded fear and anxiety, as they removed them from their comfortable home and convinced them they would die (pets and most friends won't come along).

On May 21, many believers held vigil together, waiting for God to come. Others spent the night in front of their computers, searching for news of the tell-tale earthquakes that would precede the second coming. Others went to bed, expecting to wake up in heaven. When the date passed, followers were confused. In United States, believers initially assumed that the day had to be over all over the world, and waited for midnight to fall in the last International Date Line. Harold Camping held quiet for several days; some predicted he may have committed suicide. His followers however had math and theories of their own. One was that they would have to wait 3 days, because Jesus was in his grave for three days before he rose from the dead. Some thought it must be forty days, because that is how long Noah was stranded in his Ark. Many believed they were being tested by God, to make sure their faith could hold strong among disappointment and ridicule.

When Camping was finally able to face the intact world, he explained that he was right, and his calculations were fine. He only had minor details wrong. May 21 was judgment day—a spiritual day of judgment. The physical destruction would take place months later on October 21. The failed predictions did not slow down Camping at all. At 89 years old, his radio career was stronger than ever. However, he was not, and he had a stroke only 18 days after the May 21 apocalypse failed to happen. Camping recovered well, but is still unable to speak. In March 2012, Camping made a public statement by way of his website. He made no apology, but openly acknowledged his mistakes and promised to not make end-of-the-world predictions in the future.

The address began with a positive spin, reminding followers how many people came to Christ through the campaign. "The May 21 campaign was an astounding event if you think about its impact upon this world. There is no question that millions, if not billions of people heard for the first time the Bible's warning that Jesus Christ will return. Huge portions of this world that had never read or seen a Bible heard the message the Christ Jesus is coming to rapture His people and destroy this natural world."

He then went on to admit that his date-setting was incorrect:

> Yes, we humbly acknowledge we were wrong about the timing; yet though we were wrong God is still using the May 21 warning in a very mighty way. In the months following May 21 the Bible has, in some ways, come out from under the shadows and is now being discussed by all kinds of people who never before paid any attention to the Bible.

Camping also committed to not make similar predictions in the future.

> We must also openly acknowledge that we have no new evidence pointing to another date for the end of the world. Though many dates are circulating, Family Radio has no interest in even considering another date. God has humbled us through the events of May 21, to continue to even more fervently search the Scriptures (the Bible), not to find dates, but to be more faithful in our understanding. We have learned the very painful lesson that all of creation is in God's hands and He will end time in His time, not ours! We humbly recognize that God may not tell His people the date when Christ will return, any more than He tells anyone the date they will die physically.[92]

As a result of Camping's mistakes, Family Radio faced severe financial consequences. After the incorrect prediction, donations dropped by 70%, and assets dropped by over $100 million. Although the organization is not calling it quits yet, they have been forced to drop several of their FM radio stations.[93] Some former followers have taken Camping to court for the financial losses they incurred as part of his ministry. To this day, Camping maintains that he cannot be responsible for the personal choices of others.

Traits of a Narcissistic Religious Leader

Narcissism seems to be relatively obvious in well-known cults. By the time we hear about abuse, mass suicides, and other odd behaviors, the groups are usually well-established. No cult starts off by advertising the long-term plan, but instead is covert and seems to offer members something special. In Harold Camping's case, he was not flashy (some say he wore the same five suits in 2011 that he wore during the 1970s) and he never asked anyone to hurt themselves directly, but his followers lost their jobs and families to further his agenda. In an article published in *Psychology Today*, former FBI agent Joe Navarro wrote:

> Having studied at length the life, teachings, and behaviors of Jim Jones (Jonestown Guyana), David Karesh (Branch Davidians), Stewart Traill (The Church of Bible Understanding), Charles Manson, Shoko Asahara (Aum Shinrikyo), Joseph Di Mambro (The Order of the Solar Temple aka Ordre du Temple Solaire), Marshall Heff Applewhit (Heaven's Gate), Bhagwan Rajneesh (Rajneesh Movement), and Warren Jeffs (polygamist leader), what stands out about these individuals is that they were or are all pathologically narcissistic. They all have or had an over-abundant belief that they were special, that they and they alone had the answers to problems, and that they had to be revered. They demanded perfect loyalty from followers, they overvalued

themselves and devalued those around them, they were intolerant of criticism, and above all they did not like being questioned or challenged. And yet, in spite of these less than charming traits, they had no trouble attracting those who were willing to overlook these features.

A narcissistic religious leader will have several traits of narcissism. The following pages contain examples of how narcissistic traits appear in a religious setting. Although narcissistic leaders are found in a variety of religions, in the United States, the religions are typically some form of Christianity. I use the word *minister* to describe the narcissistic religious leader, but such leaders go by many titles.

Superficial Charm. The narcissistic minister is always charming and well-liked, at least initially. He is charismatic and seems to understand others. His confidence and answers to big problems make people want to follow him. Leaders often know the specific type of followers they want, and appeal to them.

Grandiosity. The narcissistic minister has a grandiose idea of who he is, and what he can achieve. In some cases, this may be manifested as God talking or working directly through him. Many religious leaders feel a sense of direct connection with God or a higher power, but healthy leaders believe that others can have the same experiences. Narcissistic leaders believe their connection to God is unique. This is often coupled with fantasies of unlimited success, power, or brilliance. He is likely to be arrogant and haughty. When criticized, the narcissistic minister may become extremely angry. A common tactic is to view the opposition as *the enemy*. He may preach that people who question his motives or the church as a whole, or the church's connection to a higher power is *the enemy.* A narcissistic minister will also spend a great deal of time addressing these *enemies,* warning the congregation and coaching on how to deal with it.

Attention and admiration seeking: The narcissistic minister requires excessive admiration from his followers. He wears expensive or theatrical clothing, jewelry and drives an expensive car. He enjoys theatrics during church, and using over-dramatic speech. He may arrive late in order to make an entrance. At the same time, he may be hyper-sensitive to the way he is perceived by others. This is usually projected onto his family, associates and congregation, rather than his own behavior.

Power Seeking. A power-seeking minister takes an intrusive role in the lives of his members, and may dictate the way they do every day things. The narcissistic minister may see himself as a god or god-like, promoting his own glory and righteousness. In extreme cases, a narcissistic minister demands obedience from his congregation. This can include isolating members from their family and requiring that they live in certain places or move to a faraway location. Although communal living has benefits, the narcissistic minister employs it as a power device. Healthy communal living, for example, is meant to create benefits from the community, not threaten or cut-off contact from loved ones.

Kris Anderson is a Christian Marriage and Family Therapist in southern California. Because he works first-hand with pastors and their wives in his private practice, he understands the methods used by narcissistic ministers to take control. "One thing I see quite a bit in the church is something carried forward from the 'Shepherding movement' of the 1980s. Church members don't marry, buy property or make major life decisions without approval of the pastor. Church members are often pressured to commit to serve in several ministries, attend several services each week and put the desires of the pastor to grow the church above the needs of their families. Resistance to the ever increasing demands of the pastor is renounced from the pulpit as 'rebellion' or not obeying the Holy Spirit, and people are sometimes humiliated by the pastor who reveals their personal secrets and struggles by using their issues as sermon illustrations thinly veiled as a teaching topic."

Entitlement. The narcissistic minister expects to be treated as special. A sense of entitlement may lead to bending rules and breaking laws, such as sleeping with members of the church, or tax evasion. Many scandals that come out of churches begin because the minister believed he was above the law. When the narcissistic minister is caught, he often lies, denies, or passes the blame. Every minister makes human mistakes, but healthy leaders are able to come humbly to their congregation.

Exploitativeness. Exploitation in a church can range from minor to extreme abuse. Determining exploitative money practices can be tricky, because most churches and religious groups depend on donations from the members to pay church employees, buy supplies, and pay for rent. While some churches keep collection boxes quietly in the back, plenty of healthy churches pass a basket or teach sermons on financial giving. An exploitative minster, however, will ask for money, even when it puts members at financial risk. Asking members to sell all their possessions, and quit their jobs, or give money to a point of being unable to meet basic needs is typically narcissistic. A church that requires money to move up in the church is similarly exploitative. Exploitative minister may also ignore the emotional and physical needs of members. While fasting is an important part of many religions, healthy leaders recognize the needs of their congregation and would not risk a person's health for religious purposes. Any minister who has a sexual relationship with a member of the congregation is exploiting the sexual partner. Most world religions promote chastity outside of marriage, even among historically polygamous groups. In extreme groups, sex with the leader is a requirement and passed off as a rite or part of a ritual. This is always exploitative.

Devaluing others. Not only does the narcissistic minister see himself as superior, he views others an incapable or unworthy. He may subject his members to ridicule or humiliation by publically confessing their sins, discussing their weaknesses, or using them as examples. He has trouble listening to others and understanding their needs.

An Ordinary Church and an Ordinary Narcissist.

Beverly Jansen has been a pastor's wife for more than forty years. She and her husband, Pete are the quintessential church leaders. They are kind, generous and accepting, and they've raised four children who are thriving, happy adults. Their marriage is solid, and they have friends all over the country.

In the late 1960s, the Indiana church that the Jansens worked to grow was a small Bible study, mostly made up of unmarried college students. Doug Scott was a seminary student, studying to be a minister. He joined the small study. Beverly described Doug, a former hockey player, as "a big man, quick, intense, and competitive. He was driven by anger and intimidating, even after becoming a Christian." Beverly remembers that relationships with Doug usually involved manipulation and intimidation. She remembers that he would take complete advantage of people for their money and possessions, and expected others to drop everything to do what he wanted immediately. For example, he asked a church elder for his expensive Rolex watch, stating that he could use it more. When a church in a different town asked Doug to teach a mid-week Bible study, he said he would, only if the church purchased him a new car. They agreed. On several occasions, Doug used church funds for personal expenses, although he was able to make people believe they were related to the ministry. For example, his kitchen remodel was so that could host church dinners, and the addition he added to his home, was so that visiting elders would have a comfortable place to stay.

One church elder advised Pete that when in a meeting with Doug, to never say yes, but to only say *no* or *I'll get back to you on that.* He explained that if Doug was told yes, he would take advantage of everyone in the room. The problems became so serious, that the church paid thousands of dollars for Doug's therapy. He quit every therapist and never got help. How could someone so toxic continue in ministry? "When he graduated seminary, it was obvious that he was very gifted in evangelism," explained Beverly. "Every sermon ended with an emphasis on coming to Jesus *now*. The church grew—

we had new members every week. People wanted to be a part of what Doug was doing."

Doug's toxicity began to poison his personal relationships, too. The Jansens were close friends with the Scotts—they lived on the same street, their children played together, and they spent holidays together in the Jansen's vacation home overlooking Lake Michigan. Doug demanded that Beverly baby-sit, and carpool the children to school, but never reciprocated. When the church hosted a group of Japanese exchange students, Doug treated his student as a baby-sitter and house cleaner.

Beverly says that on several occasions, she would complain to Pete about Doug's behavior, but he "didn't see it." She remembers one winter; the two families spent Christmas at the lake house. Doug announced that he was on vacation, and asked Beverly to care for him and his wife's new baby so he could sleep in. Beverly agreed, and was up with the baby at five the next morning. She remembers that the baby would not stop crying. She changed her, tried to feed her, rocked her, but nothing worked. After two hours of caring for a baby whose parents were sleeping close by, Doug came flying down the stairs in a rage, the veins in his neck bulging. Beverly remembers being frightened for her life.

Another time, Beverly's sister was visiting from out of state, and the two women planned to take their children to the lake for the day. They had their car packed, and Beverly was in the kitchen grabbing last-minute snacks when Doug walked into her house, calling for her. When he found her, he demanded that she give him a haircut. She apologized, and explained that she and her sister were about to leave, but he refused to take no for an answer. Beverly's sister, who had no idea what had been going on, was horrified. She kept telling him no, but he refused to leave. He pulled a chair from the dining room table, found scissors, and sat down. He told her he would not let her leave until she was done. When she saw the veins in his neck begin to bulge—the sign that a scene was coming—she gave in, and quickly cut his hair so she could leave.

Shortly after the haircut incident, Beverly began to back away from her friendship with the Scotts. Still, it was hard to convince Pete. He says now, more than 30 years later, it is easy to see that he made mistakes. One of Pete's personal strengths—the thing that makes him a great minister, is that he is a peacemaker. He explained that he *did* take Beverly's complaints seriously, and had many long talks with Doug. Doug never apologized; instead he told Pete that he needed him as a friend and a mentor and *needed* him to balanced him out and keep him on track. Pete was confident he was doing the right thing for his church and as a Christian. One day, Beverly calmly told Pete that she was leaving him. The announcement did not come as a reaction to a crisis, but realization that she was being abused. Pete was blindsided at first, but when he realized how seriously Doug's behavior impacted his own family, he took steps to rebuild his marriage, end the friendship and eventually remove Doug from the church.

Years later, Beverly was 46 years old and diagnosed with stage four breast cancer. She was given a year to live. She and her husband met with several spiritual leaders from the community, all of whom had been a part of Pete's church throughout the years. Beverly explained, "Several of the men were very prophetic, they all came from different churches and didn't know each other well, but they had all been at the church at one time or another under Doug Scott."

During the prayer session, several of the men told Beverly that someone had put a spiritual attack on her. They all agreed Doug Scott had put a curse on her. Beverly explained to me that by *curse* she didn't mean the type of curse that is typically related to witchcraft. She meant it is an "underlying element of anger and bitterness, like *cursing* under your breath when you see someone you can't stand to be around." The group prayed for two hours, and Beverly says it worked. "I'm alive. Several of the women I worked with were diagnosed at the same time some case were less severe. They all died, I am the only one left." Beverly was dealing with a unique combination of feelings. Like all people fighting cancer, she was scared, but she was also dealing with the anger and confusion of being *cursed* by a man of God. She prayed, "This is not fair, Lord. I'm angry. I'm angry that you used Doug to cause harm to other people. You put him in a position of leadership and he intimidated his staff to where nobody could step up to him." Beverly's prayer turned into a serious discussion with God. "I listed out people who had been intimidated by Doug and left the church. *Lord how would you let this happen? You need to remove him from ministry.* God asked me how many people will be in heaven because Doug led them to the lord. The answer was thousands! Then God asked me how many will go to heaven because of me. I knew that God made him that way on purpose. Doug knows how to penetrate into people, find their fear and present the answer as Jesus Christ. God places Doug in spots where he can use his narcissistic traits. He only feels fulfilled when he can find a person's weakness and share the gospel. Everyone's gift has a good side and a bad side."

More than seven years after defeating breast cancer, Beverly and Pete were listening to a radio program that featured a psychologist discussing narcissism. The couple was riveted. "The psychologist said that what is unique about narcissists is they have an ability to discover a person's weakness in their personality, then they use that to their advantage. Narcissists affect everyone in the same way, but it never looks the same because everyone is different and has a different weakness." After listening to a clinical list of narcissistic traits, Beverly and Pete agreed that Doug was a narcissist.

Who Follows a Narcissistic Leader?

After understanding the traits of narcissistic leader, it seems like it should be easy to get away. Who would leave their lives for Harold Camping's ridiculous math calculations? How could a smart woman, like Beverly, let Doug Scott push her around? How could a loving husband like Pete stand by while his wife is being mistreated? The anecdotal belief is that such people are *weak*. This is a popular theory to explain people who join cults. They are too *weak-minded* to see right from wrong or to stand up for themselves. Believing that a victimized follower is weak is a failure to understand how the narcissist operates in interpersonal relationships. Followers of narcissistic leaders are not weak people as much as narcissists are tuned into weaknesses of others. Beverly told me that "Doug poked holes and pushed buttons to know a person's weakness." Narcissists use several tactics to keep people under control, and the tactics vary, depending on the weakness of the victim.

- **Buildup, and tear down** consists of building a person up to find out what their weaknesses are so they can be torn down. The build-up stage is very important for building a bond, and makes the victim feel loved and cared for. This pseudo-bond leaves the victim vulnerable, and when the "tear-down" occurs, the victim is emotionally vested in repairing the damage.

- **Uncertainty** is a tactic that involves rarely giving a straight answer. Vague responses create long periods of uncertainty for the victim, so that trust is built though insinuation. When the narcissist blows up, he will feel better and not understand why his victim is struggling. He may ask, "What happened? Is something wrong?" and act if he has no idea there is a problem. Once trust is destroyed, the narcissist will build it again, only to tear down once more. In religious settings, this is only done with people closest to the narcissistic minister. Beverly and Pete went through this cycle several times, as they never knew what to expect from their friendship with Doug, and were made to feel weak and stupid when they had an emotional response to his behavior.

- **Double-binding** is essentially when the narcissist says "just leave if you don't like it." Although the victim *can* usually leave at any time, they have strong emotional or even physiological ties that keep them in place. For example, a man who has sold his home and quit his job for a religious movement is *not* truly free to leave at any time.

- **Projection** is simply when the narcissist deals with his own feelings by dumping them on someone else. Oftentimes, they ask questions which often reflect their own weaknesses. For example, a minister dealing with a doubtful member may ask, "Don't you have faith?" In the narcissistic church, the minister will project his wishes onto God. *God wants to give me a car, quitting your job will enhance the Kingdom of heaven.*

- **Judgment** is a common tactic in the narcissistic church. The minister judges people harshly. He tells people, or leads them to believe they are not good Christians (or members of other religions) if they do not do as he says. In some situations, he may covertly present a judgmental sermon directed at a specific individual.

- **Sneak attacks** are verbal games used to disguise a sharp tongue. This includes preceding a statement with a phrase such as "I don't mean to interrupt" or "I don't mean to be rude, but..."These statements are often used in a kind, soft tone.

- **Cutting off communication** often begins subtly. They may ask a question and cut off the victim before they can answer. They also may ask a question designed to ignite hurt feelings or discomfort, such as "are you still having a hard time controlling your daughter?"

Cognitive Dissonance and Confirmation Bias

Aside from understanding that even healthy people can be manipulated by narcissistic leaders, two other psychological phenomena further explain the reasons that people get caught up in narcissistic ministries. The first is cognitive dissonance and the other is confirmation bias.

Back in 1844, William Miller convinced as many as 100,000 people that the world would end in a fiery blaze before March 21. When the date came and went, Miller changed the date three times before admitting he was wrong, although, much like Camping, he never apologized. On the final try, dubbed the "Great Disappointment," thousands of followers waited together for Jesus to come. Just like Harold Camping did over a hundred years later, Miller holed up in his room for days. And just like doomsday followers in 2011, the Millerites developed theories that prevented them from admitting failure—everything from an invisible coming, to a symbolic closing of salvation's door. Although many followers left the movement, it was not dead and eventually evolved into the Seventh-Day Adventist Church, which still has 15 million members today.

Cognitive dissonance occurs when a person holds two contradictory beliefs. In extreme cases, like the Millerites or Harold Camping followers, the contradictory beliefs are "God will return on this specific day" and "The prior two predictions are wrong, this one will be wrong, too." For Pete and Beverly Jansen, the contradictory beliefs were "Doug is a Godly man and an effective leader" and "Doug is an abusive, destructive man." Holding two contradictory beliefs causes anxiety, depression, frustration, guilt, embarrassment and sometimes physical illness. When faced with this predicament, people often alter one belief or reduce the importance of another, in order to continue believing both. If the stakes are really high—like eternal damnation, the person is likely to make a more dramatic choice. Also, when an individual has made major decisions—such as ending an important relationship or leaving a job, they feel they cannot afford any doubt.

Similarly, confirmation bias is the tendency to only believe information that confirms or supports existing beliefs. Once an individual has a set of beliefs, they can usually find some type of community to support them. Average people do this all the time when it comes to politics and religion, and the phenomenon only gets stronger when stakes are higher. Pete, for example, was already convinced that Doug was a Godly man and faithful minister, so he had very difficult time accepting contradictory information.

Narcissism and the Religious Individual

Narcissistic people have used the Bible to gain control over others for years. Slave owners, for example, used verses to justify control over their slaves. Historically, and still today, men use religion as a tool to control their wives. A religious narcissist uses divine text (whether it be the Bible or writings from a different religion) to further his own agenda.

- **Authority.** The religious narcissist is extremely devoted to his religious group, even dogmatic at times. He knows the religion well, and can easily quote scripture or text. He can usually back up any position or opinion with scripture, and uses that to prove his connection with God. They do not apologize, even in rare instances when admitting an error.

- **Superiority.** Religious narcissists are often solid and genuine in their beliefs, but are rigid, confrontational and judgmental. He openly criticizes, condemns, and judges others and believes he is doing them a service or his duty by pointing out shortcomings. They have a strong sense of right and wrong, with no middle ground (hint: they are always right).

- **Exhibitionism.** The religious narcissist *shows* how devoted he is by quoting scripture, attending services, and putting emphasis on rites, rituals and ceremonies. He likes to be the center of attention, at least long enough to let everyone know how devoted he is. He may volunteer to lead prayer, but likely won't get involved in behind-the-scenes work.

- **Exploitativeness.** The religious narcissist will use his knowledge of scripture to control and hurt others. This is most pronounced when controlling—and sometimes abusing wives and children, but can be used in many religious settings.

Unfortunately, narcissists in a religious setting tend to "get away with it" for longer than in other settings because the religious community wants to give people the benefit of the doubt. When a religious narcissist seems to have a strong faith, the faithful community does not want to do anything to deter that person and others from their path. Also, people in ministry are often confused by the contributions made by narcissists. Nearly thirty years after their ordeal, Beverly and Pete Jansen agree that Doug helped far more people than he hurt. They say he only hurt the people closest to him, and most members of the church were never affected by his narcissistic behavior. Their daughter, Grace believes that Doug was unable to love; in fact, he never told his own children that he loved them. Still, he was able to tell people that God loved them, which is the goal of ministry. To a close friend or family member, this is extremely hurtful, but to the public, it can make a real difference in ministry.

Part 4

IS RESISTANCE FUTILE?

Chapter 10

WHAT NEXT?

---

*"Psychology cannot tell people how they ought to live their lives.
It can however, provide them with the means for effecting personal
and social change."*

– Albert Bandura, *Social Learning Theory*

*"Time itself is neutral; it can be used either destructively or constructively.
More and more I feel that the people of ill will have used time much more
effectively than have the people of good will. We will have to repent in this
generation not merely for the hateful words and actions of the bad people but
for the appalling silence of the good people. Human progress never rolls in
on wheels of inevitability; it comes through the tireless efforts of men willing
to work to be co-workers with God, and without this hard work, time itself
becomes an ally of the forces of social stagnation. We must use time creatively,
in the knowledge that the time is always ripe to do right."*

– Martin Luther King Jr., *Why We Can't Wait*

In this book, we have discussed two different, but interrelated problems: rising narcissism in society, and narcissistic individuals. Here, we will explore *what can be done* to stop the growth of narcissism. That's a tall order, of course, and will require a social movement. We've all heard that the first step in stopping a problem is to admit there is a problem. The following social movements are in varying degrees of maturity, but are the keys to curing cultural narcissism.

A Movement to Slow Materialism

Interestingly, the recent mortgage crisis and recession that followed did little to curb materialism. Home loans are more difficult to secure, but commercial credit is still available. Americans will continue to live beyond their means as long as they believe the material items they own are more important than financial health. In 2009, the Washington Post reported that as many as 45% of homeless people living in D.C. have cell phones and laptops. Many homeless people blog about their experiences.[94] Studies in other metropolitan areas have found similar results. Not too long ago, the homeless used pay phones and the library to keep in touch, and look for work or housing. Most of the articles examining this trend refer to such technology as a "necessity." To me, this is an obvious reflection of our materialistic values. Technology certainly makes life easier for everyone, but humanity managed without this "necessity" for thousands of years. If materialism is to slow, we need to think seriously about what is *necessity* and what is a luxury.

A Movement to Recognize What We Have in Common

In 1964, Walt Disney contributed four unique attractions to the New York World's Fair. Among these was "It's a Small World" a fifteen minute interior boat voyage that allows visitors to see more than 300 animatronic dolls dressed as children from around the world. Each room depicts a different country or culture, and the children sing the same song in their own language. The Sherman brothers, who famously composed Disney's most memorable songs, wrote "It's a small world after all" as a theme of unity and peace. UNICEF requested that the song not be copyrighted so that the song could be played all over the globe. Today, it is one of the most performed and widely translated songs in the world.

Today, as individual uniqueness becomes a value more than community sameness, we lose touch with the commonalities we all share. In fact, being the same has turned into a bad thing. Parents give their children unusual names to ensure their uniqueness. Today more than ever, individuals tend to describe themselves as "spiritual, not religious" to explain a unique belief system. Teens "talk" to friends all day, without leaving their bedroom. And, it in the name of self-esteem, children are told they are special. Historically, all interpersonal relationships have started with what two people have in common. Small children play games together, adult friends like the same activities, romantic partners share the same values, co-workers share the same trade or industry, and church members share the same beliefs. If we can connect with others in a meaningful way, we can begin a move toward overcoming a culture of vanity and self-promotion.

A Movement to Remove Attention from Malignant Attention-Seekers

Americans were still reeling from the April 15, 2013 Boston Marathon bombing when *Rolling Stone Magazine* placed a sympathetic, even sexy picture of bombing suspect Dzhokhar Tsarnaev. Tsarnaev was responsible for killing three people, wounding more than 200, and creating a frantic man-hunt that put the city of Boston in a state of terror and resulted in the death of a police officer. The photo, which looked eerily similar to one of Jim Morrison, featured on a 1991 Rolling Stone cover, created controversy. Why was a killer's face in a spot normally reserved for musicians and pop stars? Many people felt it was wrong to give such attention to a criminal terrorist. Pharmacy chain CVS, among others, refused to sell the issue in stores. Not all violent criminals get their picture on the cover of a glamorous rock magazine, but the sensational criminals do get their names and faces on newspapers, news websites, Twitter, and television news programs. If they're lucky, they even get a snappy nickname (The Aurora, Colorado movie theater shooter has been dubbed *The Batman Killer*).

When it comes down to it, anyone who commits a violent crime or even a suicide in a public place wants attention. In an op-ed for the *New York Times*, Roger Ebert wrote:

> I think the link is between the violence and the publicity. Those like James Holmes, who feel the need to arm themselves, may also feel a deep, inchoate insecurity and a need for validation. Whenever a tragedy like this takes place, it is assigned catchphrases and theme music, and the same fragmentary TV footage of the shooter is cycled again and again. Somewhere in the night, among those watching will be another angry, aggrieved loner who is uncoiling toward action[95]

By turning violent criminals into celebrities, we send a clear message to the next up-and-coming criminal that his fifteen minutes of fame are up for grabs.

A Movement to Protect our Children

Although narcissism in the media is not going anywhere, parents can help the epidemic by paying attention to what their children watch and listen to, and discuss narcissistic images whenever possible. Often, in children's shows, self-absorbed characters are repellent to adults, but it may not be obvious to young children, intent to copy everything they see without context (if you've ever been embarrassed by a toddler, you know what I mean). Bad messages will come and go (my guilty pleasure right now is enjoying Pretty Little Liars with my teenage daughter; this book and television series is grounded on vanity, back-stabbing, lies and secrets) and it's okay to indulge on occasion, but it is important to encourage our children to watch movies and read books centered on teamwork, friendship, and overcoming problems, both ordinary and extraordinary. This seemed to be the norm when I was growing up (Thanks, Judy Blume!) and can still be found. For example, *The Harry Potter Series*, and the *Hunger Games Series* of both books and films center on characters that are smart, strong, work hard, and work with others to overcome unspeakable evil.

Parents also need to be committed to not promoting narcissism in their child-rearing practices. This means developing appropriate expectations, and treating our children as people who are learning to be healthy adults, *not* princes and princess ready to inherit greatness.

Parents can also help by insisting that children engage in face-to-face time rather than screen-time. Whether this means banning tablets, or setting healthy boundaries for cell phone use, kids must be exposed to traditional adult conversation and interactions as well as the effort and work that goes into traditional friendships and other relationships. After reading Chapter 3 of this book, a test reader said, "I definitely was very self-involved probably through my mid-twenties before I realized that you have to put effort into friendships and relationships if you want them to be good relationships. It's weird that it took me that long and if I'm being completely honest, it still takes effort, it doesn't come easy. Like if a friend will ask a favor, I'll be thinking *fuck no I'd rather blow my brains out,* but I'll usually actually say *yeah, no problem* because if I really can make it work, then it would be selfish not to, and if it were me, I'd want them to say yes. Maybe I'm a self-involved person who tries hard not to be, but because of that realization in my mid-twenties I have much better friends than a lot of people I know."

A movement to protect children from materialism and other issues symptomatic of narcissism has already begun. Author Kim John Payne wrote the book *Simplicity Parenting* based on twenty years of experience working with busy families. In addition to his books, Payne teaches seminars, hosts webinars, blogs and sells recordings that teach parents that "less is more" by focusing on a de-cluttered environment (less material objects), a predictable rhythm, a reasonable schedule (less pressure) and unplugging from media to spend more time with parents and develop social and emotional intelligence. Movements like this do not only benefit children, they give parents a perspective that relieves pressure and allows more relaxation and fun.

A Movement Toward Developing Empathy

As discussed earlier, empathy is the natural enemy of narcissism. Although empathy is decreasing, it does exist and can continue. Although there is no direct correlation between parental empathy and child empathy, parents whose children have high levels of empathy tend to be low in controlling punishment, high in warmth and responsiveness, and encourage children to explore how their behaviors affect others (for example, asking *How do you think Johnny feels when you bite him?* Rather than *Don't bite!* Or worse, biting back). A 26year-old study that examined the ways that parental attitudes shape adult behaviors also found that children whose fathers were involved in their upbringing, and whose mothers were satisfied with maternal roles and who accepted dependent behavior, were more empathetic as adults.[96]

Empathy is teachable in both children and adults. My children go to a small, but growing Waldorf school in southern California. Their school recently won an award for their Compassionate Campus Program. Compassionate campus involves matching lower grade students with upper grade buddies. The students meet with their buddies weekly to connect with each other and connect with the campus. They play together and talk, so that both older and younger students develop non-judgmental listening skills. Afterward, the older students meet with teachers to discuss school-wide social challenges. Older children develop empathy by interacting with younger children and use these skills to relate to children their own age. Since the program was implemented, discipline was reduced by 60% and children and parents both report feeling safer. Bullying is virtually non-existent, and when it crops up, is recognized and dealt with immediately.

Mindfulness is also an important step in increasing empathy and decreasing narcissistic traits in individuals. Teresa, who has been dealing with narcissistic tendencies her entire life explained:

> I've just tried to become a better person over the last 25 yrs., taking classes, joining support groups and reading tons of self-help books because I've always felt like there is something wrong with me. I know that's not really true now, and have learned some surprising things; like the fact that a *reaction* to something is really a choice. It's an automatic response, but a learned one, and it can be changed. And our memories, viewpoints/opinions are all subjective. It all depends on how we choose to look at it. And thoughts cause feelings which cause actions. And thoughts can be changed. Anyway, I think I'm a better mother, wife and friend now than I was in my 20s, for sure. Experience is a good teacher.

Treatment for NPD

Although no magic pill for narcissism exists, several therapeutic treatments are known to make a difference in the lives of narcissists and their families. Unfortunately, narcissists rarely realize they have a problem because they tend to blame others. Most people with NPD do not seek treatment until they have a personal crisis. The two most common reasons a person with NPD seeks treatment is serious relationship problems, such as being left by a spouse or being unable to maintain a relationship; and losing a job or other important opportunity, usually due to angry or aggressive behavior. Under these conditions, the narcissist expects a quick solution and rarely wants to deal with the discomfort and work of long-term therapy. Once therapy starts, narcissistic traits often find their way into the therapeutic relationship. The narcissist may think he is more capable than the therapist, devaluation or jealousy of the therapist may occur. If the therapy is required, for example, the result of a court order, the narcissist may be so intent on manipulating the therapist that a healthy relationship does not develop. A somatic narcissist may use sexuality to deflect from the issues at hand.

No matter why a person develops NPD, the behaviors are all *learned* responses to a variety of emotional situations, and although challenging, new behaviors can be learned to replace the old ones, and hopefully, the new behaviors will elicit positive responses in loved ones, even if they do not come naturally. The following techniques are used to treat NPD:

Cognitive Behavioral Therapy is one of the most common therapy methods used today. It involves changing cognitions that impact behavior, and often changing behaviors before the cognition can be changed. For example, if a man with NPD can commit to not interrupting his co-workers, he may find that they enjoy being with him more. This positive interaction may change the way he thinks about his co-workers, and he may consistently behave in a pro-social way. Another goal of cognitive behavioral therapy is to realize that individuals can control how they perceive other people and situations. This can be very difficult for a person who engages in black-and-white thinking or externalizing blame.

Psychoanalysis is the traditional Freudian method of individual therapy that elicits an image of lying on a couch, discussing childhood trauma. Although it may be a caricature in modern culture, psychoanalysis can be useful in the long-term treatment of NPD. The goal of psychoanalysis is to reduce the conflicts that occur between the unconscious and conscious mind. Psychoanalysis gives the narcissist plenty of opportunities to talk about himself, as it is client-driven, but may take several years (and thousands of dollars) for progress to be evident. This treatment method is most appropriate for the narcissist who genuinely wants to explore his sense of self and improve his life and outlook over time.

Dialectical Behavior Therapy has historically been used to treat Borderline Personality Disorder, but is also useful in treating NPD. Dialectical behavior therapy focuses on mindfulness, emotional regulation, distress tolerance, and interpersonal effectiveness. These areas are important, because improving them can reduce narcissistic symptoms as well as personal suffering or discomfort, without the patient needing to admit to or understand his diagnosis.

Group Therapy. The very nature of NPD makes group therapy unappealing to the narcissist. Narcissist will resist, not wanting to share the spotlight, or not believing another person could understand their struggles. Still, group therapy provides narcissists with opportunities to practice social skills, respect others, and listen to an authority in a microcosm. The most common reason a narcissist joins group therapy is as a result of a legal order, such as being required to join an anger management group or alcohol group. It is important that a narcissist is in an appropriate group setting. When placed with non-narcissists, he may be prone to taking over the group or manipulating other group members.

Psychiatric Medications and Substance Abuse Treatment. There is no drug that targets NPD, but many prescription drugs can reduce anxiety, depression, and poor impulse control which can make life more tolerable for the narcissist. Because more than half of people diagnosed with NPD also deal with substance abuse, treatment is very important. Some narcissists seek treatment for substance abuse, before, or instead of treatment for NPD. A person with NPD may think that he is above addiction, at the same time wanting to feel better or feel numb. 12-step programs, such as Alcoholics Anonymous and Narcotics Anonymous can be useful in breaking through denial, but narcissists are prone to dominating group settings. They may attend for the audience rather than to change behavior. Although substance abuse treatment alone will not do much to change NPD symptoms, it is an important component of treatment.

A Matter of Perspective

It's not fair to tell you about narcissism and convince you that it's a problem without letting you know that there is a different side. Among a huge pile of books, articles, and studies that show that narcissism and the problems it entails is growing, was a 2007 article that challenged everything I believe about the Millennial Generation and the future of our narcissistic society. Entitled, "From the Me Decade to the Me Millenium: The Cultural History of Narcissism," Imogen Tyler explains the ways that narcissism as a label has been used to keep down women and minorities, stigmatizing sexual and social groups. Tyler points out that narcissism has been a cultural concern since the 1970s, a time that came to be known as the "me decade." This awakening was the result of an article written by Tom Wolfe and published in the August 23, 1976 edition of *New York Magazine*. In his article, Wolfe characterized older Americans as hard-working, ambitious, sacrificing and devoted, while the current generation of the time only cared about self-gratification. To make his point, Wolfe used narratives of several fictitious characters, including a sex-obsessed business woman. Wolfe explains that this woman, who he calls a "sexual princess," is nothing without her sexuality. He goes on to describe her lying on a banquet hall floor, moaning and screaming. He sums up his view of women by saying, "The great unexpected dividend of the feminist movement has been to elevate an ordinary status – woman, housewife – to the level of drama. One's very existence as a woman ... as Me ... becomes something all the world analyzes, agonizes over, draws cosmic conclusions from, or, in any event, takes seriously."[97] Wolfe is loud and clear in his belief that a woman's desire to be treated as an equal and be taken seriously as a human being is a symptom of pathological narcissism.

Around the same time, author Christopher Lasche was happy to agree with Wolfe. In his 1978 book, *The Culture of Narcissism*, Lasche is clear that narcissism is the enemy of masculinity and the patriarchal family. Any deviation from this tradition, such as working women, homosexual men, or even men who do not drip of "rugged masculinity" was narcissistic. As for women, he said that narcissism within our culture "requires that women smoke and drink in public, move about freely, and assert their right to happiness instead of living for others."[97] Lasche did not stop at insulting women. He also explained that "The white middle-class family is being infected by the ghetto."[97] In previous writings, he attributed narcissism to the rise in "ghetto culture" which included gang violence, drug use and other crime.

I admit that exploring narcissism has an embarrassing history. Tyler ended her article by saying, "If we are to continue to draw on the meta-psychology of narcissism in theoretical accounts of cultural change, we must therefore critically interrogate the politics of narcissism."[97] Tyler is completely correct. Today, ending narcissism has no political agenda. Social scientists who are concerned with changing cultural norms are not interested in holding anyone back, including the millennial generation. Today's anti-narcissism movement isn't about alienating any specific group, or stifling technological growth. If anything, we want to see our children reach adulthood in a healthy, thriving world.

Joel Stein ended his 2013 article entitled "Milennials: The Me Me Me Generation" by saying, "So, yes, we have all that data about narcissism and laziness and entitlement. But a generation's greatness isn't determined by data; it's determined by how they react to the challenges that befall them. And, just as important, by how we react to them. Whether you think millennials are the new greatest generation of optimistic entrepreneurs or a group of 80 million people about to implode in a dwarf star of tears when their expectations are unmet depends largely on how you view change. Me, I choose to believe in the children. God knows they do." As for me, I believe that people are still capable of empathy and still want social connections. I believe these people—whether by choice or as a result of catastrophe—will start the social movement to stop narcissism in its tracks.

Chapter 11

A HAPPY ENDING? INTERVIEW WITH THE NARCISSIST

When you meet Lucas Oliver, the first thing you will notice is his huge smile and great teeth. He is immediately warm and welcoming. What I remember about Lucas Oliver is that when he was my high school drama teacher, he made us perform the plays he wrote. During my senior year, he cast himself in a student production of *Macbeth*. In high school, we all knew the fun and energetic drama teacher was full of himself, but it was more than fifteen years later that I learned he had been clinically diagnosed with narcissistic personality disorder.

Lucas is not shy about discussing his diagnosis or what that means for himself and his family. He invited me to his home for our interview and immediately opened up. The oldest of three sons in a traditional Catholic household, Lucas's father was the head of the family, and his mother was "simple and nice." Lucas has always known that he was a narcissist, although he didn't have a word for it as a child. Since toddlerhood, he felt like a "selfish person" and believed his needs were more important than the needs of others. He shared an early memory of being responsible for teaching his youngest brother to roller skate, but leaving him so he could skate alone. He knew it was wrong, but did it anyway. Lucas explained that religion regulated most of his impulses as a child, but when his youngest brother was sexually abused by a priest, he turned away from the church and his family. He experienced strong feelings of shame and disgust, to the point of not wanting friends to meet his family, visit his house, or learn of his brother's abuse. Losing his religion also meant losing his only method for regulating his impulses. A rigid sense of right and wrong had kept him striving for, or at least recognizing, goodness.

Lucas' impulse control problems intensified as he grew older. By high school, he was smoking pot and drinking, and he was an alcoholic before graduating college. Narcissism is often characterized by a strong sense of being above the rules. This has been true of Lucas' life. He was arrested for driving under the influence of alcohol when he was 21, but continued to drink and drive for years. He explained that he knew it was dangerous and wrong, but didn't care. Despite "not caring," this time in his life was characterized by intense anxiety. "I can remember a period in my teenage years where I didn't give a fuck about anything other than smoking dope, drinking, and trying to get to third base. Home plate was too intense. Too much fear. Catholic guilt and quite honestly I couldn't understand the angle of approach with a penis and vagina in the traditional position or any position. I hated geometry. The same thing with kissing. If I didn't understand it I was afraid or rather if I didn't feel comfortable I didn't have confidence. So I shielded away."

During early adulthood, Lucas' love life was a series of one-night stands, and he never had a serious girlfriend until he met Carrie, to whom he has now been married for over twenty years. His inability to see past his own needs interfered with dating. When he found himself becoming emotionally intimate with a woman, he sabotaged the relationship by hyper-focusing, and projecting into the future, creating anxiety and depression for himself and pushing away the potential partner. Oftentimes, he would make himself emotionally unavailable. He explained that for most of his adult life, he had a tendency to cancel plans without calling. If he didn't want to keep a commitment, he simply didn't show up. In general, Lucas wasn't a very attentive or sensitive boyfriend. "I have always felt a rebellious energy *like fuck it life is finite so why not indulge and absorb all I can?* Binding or permanent things, or relationships required work I felt disinterested in. Time is a big flaw with me in building a healthy relationship. I'd tend to just do things I want to do for *me.*"

He admitted to dealing with sex addiction, and he acted on impulses to party and go to strip clubs. He reflected that he knew his behavior was wrong, but he never took the time to look past himself. As someone who is now past that point in his life, he explained, "I laugh my ass off at men my age who are narcissistic and cheat on their wives, and say *I haven't found the right woman.* It's like talking politics with a one year old. The problem is *you!* Not to say that couples can't grow apart, but happiness is *not* finding the 'thing' that pleases or satisfies you. It's a devil's circle. Trust me. As for my wife, she endured all the fleeting attractions that I obsessed with. That narcissistic ADD combo is lethal. Throw in the moral self-condemnation and you are fucked without Vaseline. Then you self-medicate with drinking because life is fucked and then the addiction starts where being in the bar, hearing the sounds, seeing the eye candy both stimulates and helps hyper-focus then it's a love affair with being away from family. Meanwhile, you isolate yourself from family, hurt people who love you, and that starts the seeds of resentment."

Lucas and Carrie had a turbulent marriage for years. They separated several times, and as Lucas described it, "the separations ran their course." He does not know if the marriage has continued out of love or fear of change; but he did state that he wants Carrie to be happy. Lucas compared being a married narcissist to the experience of a gay person pretending to be straight. He says that he always feels single, and until recently, acted as though he was single. However, he has had no problem remembering that Carrie has made a commitment to *him.* For years, he was easily jealous, and tended to "mind read," his behavior adjusting to his predictions.

Despite Lucas's personal difficulties, his career never suffered. He described periods of feeling as though teaching was not "good enough" and having a desire to do something else. He earned his real estate license a few years ago, but lost interest once the housing market crashed. Even now, he is working on a screenplay and has started a new venture as a promoter for local bands. Despite his varied interests, Lucas has always managed to keep a stable job. He likes teaching, and his students like him. He demonstrated a genuine interest in his students, by recalling details of students' lives from decades before. When I asked Lucas how he maintained his career in spite of the boundary issues that seem to have wreaked havoc on his other interpersonal relationships, he described his coping strategy as a "Rolodex of personalities." It isn't hard to imagine an angry parent or frustrated principal being disarmed by his big, warm smile.

Becoming a father did not change Lucas's internal struggle with narcissism. Walking into Lucas's home, you would never guess that it houses a struggling family. Tastefully decorated, the walls are covered in pictures of smiling children enjoying life with their parents. Externally, he believes, he was an excellent father. He has supported his family financially, attended birthday parties and school events, but acknowledged that he did not make real changes and did not build a relationship with his teenage daughters while they were young. When I asked him how his narcissism has affected his parenting, he said,

> I Feel like I am a failure. There's a certain pressure to 'parent' and I have no fucking idea what that means. My shortcomings have been so obvious to me so I can only imagine what they have looked like to them, plus Carrie is a far better parent to them in many ways. To 'love' period has always been like a performance. I have no idea what that word means. I can only say now that I try to find moments to be real with them and honestly share what I am feeling or thinking. Same way as a husband. Love is contrary to my nature in the doing but internally it's in there. Just very difficult to express.

He also explained that he put Carrie in the position of being a single parent emotionally.

> To me, as described in therapy, I have struggled with the selfless expression of love for everyone. It's like a thing I can't express. Maybe fear based, fear of intimacy. Narcissism is not as clear cut as people see it. People think *Ah, he's a prick, or a selfish prick. He only cares about himself.* It's like when a homosexual finally comes out and says *I'm gay!* That's akin to a narcissistic person. Once a narcissist accepts that his or her sole instinctive feeling or care is primarily to himself then the rest of life can be managed because they have that insight. I have always tried to be open with my kids and when recognizing this trend I have sat down and explained that daddy is sorry. He is trying to be better. He loves you in his limited way. It's shitty, but in order to be believed one must be open and vulnerable and this is what I've tried to do. It's like love can only get so strong in action with a narcissist. The outward expression for my wife and kids is both easy and hard. One daughter is a carbon copy of me and the other is the opposite. I have always noticed the combo of narcissism and ADD in both but with one it's blatantly obvious. She's a train wreck like me to a lesser degree but the narcissism is still there. My parenting has gotten better but that's because I accept myself without judgment and treat my limitations like a behavior that has to be worked on. Thought comes in *Do this for yourself today. Go to movies, ride motorcycle*, it used to be *hit golf balls, hang out with friends and drink* . Now, it's *No motherfucker, WHAT can you do with your family OR at least see what they want to do and try and BE with them.* So in

a nutshell, being a narcissist with a family is a struggle in battling against those selfish *me, me, me* tendencies but a way more difficult, even impossible for family members if the narcissist is in denial. The only thing I have done effectively other than what I have described is to strip away the MORAL *I'm in the flesh* bullshit. The Christian explanation is that we're all pieces of shit in need of saving and of course we shoveled down impossible shit like sell everything you have, follow Jesus at any cost, pray 37 hours of the day, and never thinking of fucking anyone else cause of course by just thinking of fucking means you've fucked. Well if that was the case I would have fucked thousands more women.

Toward the end of our interview, Lucas was able to sum up his narcissism in a very real way. He told me that he can rationalize anything. Anything he wants to do, anyone he wants to hurt, he can rationalize it. If, for some reason, at the core of his being, he is unable to reconcile his behavior, he "chalks it up to a fuck up."

Everything changed for Lucas about four years ago, when he sought therapy for what he believed was adult Attention Deficit Hyperactivity Disorder (ADHD). Being diagnosed with narcissistic personality disorder (NPD) not only allowed Lucas to understand his out-of-control thoughts, feelings, and behaviors, but also the diagnosis gave him a strong foundation for change. Lucas has been able to modify his thoughts by changing his behavior. It does not always come naturally, but he has noticed that things go better for him when he can behave differently. He related that he and Carrie recently had a disagreement in which she was upset and made hurtful statements. In the past, he would argue and escalate the fight, but he gave her space and the disagreement diffused.

Lucas also explained that Buddhism has helped him to become more mindful of the needs and feelings of others and "anchor in the present." This is particularly important to his life, as he has spent most of it anticipating hell after death. As Lucas discussed his present life, the man he described bore little resemblance to the self-centered, narcissistic man we had talked about for over an hour. He seemed much more self-aware and confessed that he would not want his daughters to date a man like him. Today, Lucas' only regret is that he did not change sooner. He really seems to have it all together. He explained that he has a tense relationship with his 17-year-old daughter, Violet, who he believes has many narcissistic tendencies. Still, he expressed a sincere desire for both children to be happy and explained that he does not push academics or define himself by the success of his children.

Our interview ended as guests began arriving in Lucas and Carrie's cozy Los Angeles home for a party. He introduced me to several of his friends, explaining each of their personal and professional merits. One friend is an attorney, another, a doctor, and his cousin can get tickets to any concert, any time. Lucas friends seem to really care about him and his openness about his shortcomings was clear. He seemed truly comfortable with himself, and able to acknowledge his faults. Lucas was proof that a man with narcissistic personality disorder can have a happy marriage, well-adjusted children and a stable career. The experience gave me hope that narcissism does not have to destroy people, relationships or families.

As I was leaving the party, Carrie asked me how the interview went. Beaming, I told her that I was thrilled to have a happy ending for my book. She looked at me in surprise and said, "this is not a happy-fucking-ending."

Acknowledgements

Thank you to Erik—without you, I could do nothing.

To my children, thank you for understanding my long nights, and to my parents and grandparents, thank you for teaching me to think deeply.

Thank you to Hilly, Kristen and Melinda for helping me to defeat writer's block with humor, manicures and ridiculous stories. Erika, thank you for listening to me complain at all hours. To all my other friends who entertain me at dinner and go camping with me, your companionship and support means everything to me.

I am forever grateful to Kelly, Maura, Karla, and Tiffany. Your insight and attention to detail has helped me tremendously.

I am extremely grateful to every person who shared their story. Your capacity to help others through your pain is amazing.

About the Author

 Heather Sheafer is a freelancer and author trained in psychology. She lives in Orange County, California with her husband, three children, and two dogs. She enjoys vegetarian cooking and standup comedy. Heather received a Master of Arts degree in clinical psychology from Pepperdine University in Malibu, California. She is currently pursuing a PhD in psychology. Her next book on narcissism in relationships is due out in 2014.

INDEX

REFERENCES

1. Dingus, A. (1997). Bonnie and Clyde. *Texas Monthly.* 25(1): 224

2. Knickerbocker, B. (2013). Christoper Dorner manhunt over, but troubling issues remain. *Christian Science Monitor.* February 16, 2013

3. American Psychiatric Association. (2000). *Diagnostic and Statistical Manual of Mental Disorders* (4th ed., text rev.). Washington, DC:

4. Bardenstein, K.K. (2009). The cracked mirror: Features of Narcissistic Personality Disorder in children. *Psychiatric Annals.* 39(3): 146-155

5. Bleiberg, E. (1994). Normal and pathological narcissism in adolescence. *American Journal of Psychology.* 48(1): 30-51

6. Sawrie, S.M., Watson, P.J., Sherbak, J.F., Greene, R.L. & Arredondo, R. (1997). Alcoholism and narcissism: Assessing a presumed relationship with the MMI-2

7. Blackburn, R. (2007). Personality disorder and psychopathy: Conceptual and empirical integration. *Psychology, Crime & Law.* 13(1): 7-18

8. Summers and Summers (2006). Unadulterated Arrogance: Autopsy of the Narcissistic Parental Alienator. *American Journal of Family Therapy.* 34(5). 399-428

9. Thomaes, S., Bushman, B.J., Orobio de Castro, B. & Stegge, H. (2009). What makes narcissists bloom? A framework for research on the etiology and development of narcissism. *Development and psychopathology.* 21(4) 1233-4

10. Imbesi, Lucia. (1999). The Making of a Narcissist : *Clinical Social Work Journal,* 27, no. 1 (1999): 41-54

11. Hamilton, V. (1982). *Narcissus and Oedipus: the Children of Psychoanalysis.* London

12. Greven, D. (2009). Rereading narcissism: Freud's theory of male homosexuality and Hawthorne's "gentle boy." *Modern psychoanalysis.* 34(1)

13. Campbell, W.K & Miller, J.D. (2011). *The Handbook of Narcissism and Narcissistic Personality Disorder: Theoretical Approaches, Empirical Findings, and Treatments.* Hoboken, N.J.: John Wiley & Sons

14. Clark, L. A. (2005). Temperament as a unifying basis for personality and psychopathology. *Journal of Abnormal Psychology,* 114, 505-521.

15. Paris, J. (2013). *The Intelligent Clinician's Guide to the DSM-5.* N.Y.: Oxford

16. APA (1980). *Diagnostic and Statistical Manual of Mental Disorders,* 3rd ed.

17. American Psychiatric Association. (2013). Highlights of Changes from DSM-IV-TR to DSM-5. *American Psychiatric Publishing.*

18. Jian, Ma (2013, May 21). China's Brutal One-Child Policy. *The New York Times.*

19. McLaughlin, Kathleen. (2013, January 3). China and the worst-ever, man-made gender gap. *The Global Post*

20. Cameron, L., Erkal, N., Gangadharan, L & Meng, X. (2013). Little emperors: behavioral impacts of China's One-child policy. *Science*. 339(6122): 953-7

21. Zhang, Y., Kohnstamm, G.A., Cheung, P.C. & Lau, S. (2001). A new look at the old "little emperor": Developmental changes in the personality of only children in China. *Social Behavior & Personality: An International Journal*. 29(7): 725

22. Scelzo, T. & Lerman, D. (2009). Little emperors grown up: A case study of cosmetic usage. *Young Consumers*. 10(2) 110-119

23. Wang, Y. & Fong, V.L. (2009). Little emperors and the 4:2:1 generation: China's singletons. *Journal of the American Academy of Child and Adolescent Psychiatry*. 48(12): 1137-9

24. Twenge, J. & Foster, J. Birth cohort increases in narcisstic personality traits among American college students 1982-2009. *Social Psychological & Personality Science*. 1(1) : 99-106

25. Campbell, W.K. Miller, J.D., and Buffardi, L.E. (2010). The United States and the "Culture of Narcissism" : An examination of perception. *Social Psychology and Personality Science. 1:222*

26. Konrath, S.H., O'Brien, E. and Hsing, C. (2011). Changes in dispositional empathy in American college students over time: A meta-analysis. *Personality and Social Psychology Review* 15:180

27. Summers and Summers (2006). Unadulterated Arrogance: Autopsy of the Narcissistic Parental Alienator. *American Journal of Family Therapy*. 34(5). 399-428

28. Stein, J. (2013). Millennials: The me me me generation. May 20.

29. Berner, G. (2009). Black children, white preference: Brown v. Board, the doll tests, and the politics of self-esteem. *American*

Quarterly. 61(2) 299-332

30. Barry, C., Frick, P.J. & Killian, A.L. (2003). The relation of narcissism and self-esteem to conduct problems in children: A preliminary investigation. *Journal of Clinical Child and Adolescent Psychology.* 32(1) 139-152

31. Robinson, M. (2008). Beware the feel good curriculum - it backfires. *The Times Educational Supplement,* 4809: 36

32. Donald, B. (2013). Babies whose efforts are praised become more motivated kids, says Stanford researchers. *Stanford Report, February 12.*

33. Ginott, H.G. (1965). *Between Parent & Child.* New York, New York.

34. Estroff, Marano, H. (2013). A nation of wimps. *Psychology Today.* February 19.

35. Caplan, Hoke, Diamond & Karashenboyem. (2012). Free to choose but liable for the consequences. *Journal of Law, Medicine & Ethics*

36. Au, M. (2011). When parents don't vaccinate, I take it personally. *Psychology Today.* June 8

37. Chang, J. (2013). Toddlers and Tablets: Way of the future? *ABC News* June 5.

38. DeLoache, J., Chiong, C., Sherman, K., Islam, N., Vanderborght, Troseth, G., Strouse, G. & O'Doherty, K. (2010). Do babies learn from baby media? *Psychological Science.* 21(11) 1570-1574

39. Jones, B. (2013). LAUSD moving to next phase of iPad program. *Los Angeles Daily News.* November 12.

40. Summers, D.M & Summers, C.C. (2006). Unadulterated arrogance: Autopsy of the narcissistic parental alienator. *The American Journal of Family Therapy,* 34:5, 399-428

41. Karen, D. (2005). No child left behind? Sociology ignored! *Sociology of Education.* 78(2): 165

42. Adams, C. (2012). Most students still not college-ready, ACT report finds. *Education Week.* 32(2): 27

43. Marantz Henig, R. (2010). Why are so many people in their 20s taking so long to grow up? *New York Times Magazine.* August 18

44. Center for Innovative Public Health Research. (2011). Growing up with media: Parent and youth reported household rules characteristics.

45. Adler, Margot. (2013). The Occupy movement at 2: Many voices, many messages. *National Public Radio, September 17*

46. http://www.teaparty.org 2013.

47. Wollner, A. (2013). Public opinion toward tea party hits low point. *KPCC Southern California Public Radio.* October 16, 2013.

48. Bors, M (2013). The generation we love to dump on. *CNN.com.* July 9

49. Alsup, D. & Brumfield, B. (2013). Florida man allegedly kills wife, posts confession, photo of body on Facebook. *CNN.* September 18

50. Moya-Smith, S. (2013). Driver who said he 'killed a man' in online video officially indicted, turns self in. *NBC News.* September 9.

51. Panek, E., Nardis, Y. & Konrath, S. (2013). Mirror or megaphone? How relationships between narcissism and social networking site use differ on Facebook and Twitter.

52. Whitbourne, S.K. (2013). The high cost of facebook exhibitionism. *Psychology Today.* April

53. Watkins, D. (2012). Why you shouldn't have more than 354 Facebook friends. *Men's Health.* February

54. Slater Tate, A. (2013). When my tween son doesn't love me. *Brain Child*. November

55. Kross, E.M. Verduyn, P., Demiralp, E., Park, J., Seungiae, L.D., Lin, N., Shablack, H., Jodides, J. & Ybarra, O. Facebook Use Predicts Declines in Subjective Well-Being in Young Adults

56. Chaulk, K. & Jones, T. (2011). Online obsessive relational intrusion: Further concerns about Facebook. *Journal of Family Violence*. 26:245-254

57. Madden, M., Lennhart, A., Cortesi, S. Gasser, U., Duggan, M., Smith, A. & Beaon, M. (2013). Teens, social media and privacy. *Pew Research Center*. May 21

58. Aguilar, E. (2013). Gov. Jerry Brown signs bill increasing online privacy for minors in California. *Southern California Public Radio*. September 23

59. LaBarre, S. (2013). Why we're shutting off our online comments. *Popular Science*. September 24

60. http://www.motherjones.com/about

61. West, J. & McDonnell, T. (2013). We tracked down our biggest troll . . .and kind of liked him. *Mother Jones*. May 20

62. Young, S.M. & Pinsky, D. (2006). Narcissism and celebrity. *Journal of Research in Personality*. 40(5) 463-471

63. Covington Armstrong, S. (2012). Why I allow my daughter to wear THIS. *Huffington Post*. August 30.

64. Klara, R. (2012). Perspective: Boys keeping busy. *Ad Week* June 28

65. Bliss-Holtz, J. (2009). My beautiful mommy: Preparing children for a parent's surgery or for being a narcissist in training? *Issues in Comprehensive Pediatric Nursing* 32(4) 157-159

66. Ogden, C. L., Carroll, M. D., Kit, B.K., & Flegal, K. M. (2012). Prevalence of obesity and trends in body mass index among U.S. children and adolescents, 1999-2010. *Journal of the American Medical Association*, 307(5), 483-490.

67. Quenqua, D. (2013). Muscular body image lures boys into gym, and obsession. *New York Times*. November 19

68. Green, P. & Cellier, C. (2007). Celiac Disease Medical Progress. *The New England Journal of Medicine*. 357(17).

69. White, M. (2013). Why we're wasting billions on gluten-free food. *Time Magazine, March 13*

70. MacLean, K. (2013). Surviving Whole Foods. *Huffington Post*. September 16

71. Morrison, P. (2013). What's behind the pink of breast cancer awareness month? *The Los Angeles Times*. Oct 16

72. Bassett, L. (2010). Susan G. Komen Foundation elbows out charities over use of the word "cure." December 7

73. Wallis, D. (2012). Komen Foundation struggles to regain wide support. *The New York Times*. November 8

74. Kaufman, S.B. (2011). The Peacock paradox. *Psychology Today*. 44(4) 56-63

75. Akhatar, S. (2009). Love, Sex and Marriage in the Setting of a Pathological Narcissism. *Psychiatric Annals, 39(2). 185-193*

76. Rubinstein, G. (2010). Narcissism and self-esteem among homosexual and heterosexual male students. *Journal of Sex & Marital Therapy*. 36(1) 24-34

77. Drescher, J. (2010). There is no there there: A discussion of narcissism and self-esteem among homosexual and heterosexual male students. 36(1): 38-47

78. Cohen, O. (1998). Parental narcissism and the disengagement of the non-custodial father after divorce. *Clinical Social Work Journal.* 26(2).

79. Chappel, K. (2000). Richard Williams: Venus and Serena's father whips the pros and makes his family number 1 in tennis. *Ebony.* 55(8).

80. Intini, J. (2009). Richard Williams, Venus and Serena's famous father, on creating champions, his critics, parenting and the problems with tennis. *Maclean's* 122(34) p. 14

81. Brown, Nina. (2008). *Children of the Self-Absorbed: A Grown-Up's Guide to Getting Over Narcissistic Parents.* New Harbinger Publications.

82. Fahlgren, S. (1991). Cheerleader Case: The Ultimate Stage Mother? *Los Angeles Times.* March 17, 1991.

83. Hewitt, B. (1991). Murderous Intent. *People, September 23, 1991.* 36(11)

84. Lang, A. & Mascia, K. (2012). The Texas cheerleader case: A daughter's painful journey. *People.* February 20, 2012. 77(8)

85. Meier, P.D., Cherlebois, L. and Munz, C. (2011). *You Might Be a Narcissist If...: How to Identify Narcissism in Ourselves and Others and What We Can Do About It.* Langdon Street Press, Minneapolis, MN

86. Young, S.M. & Pinsky, D. (2006). Narcissism and celebrity. *Journal of Research in Personality.* 40(5) 463-471

87. Cohen, O. (1998). Parental narcissism and the disengagement of the non-custodial father after divorce. Clinical Social Work. 26(2).

88. Summers and Summers (2006). Unadulterated Arrogance: Autopsy of the Narcissistic Parental Alienator. *American Journal of Family Therapy.* 34(5). 399-428

89. Galambos, N., Barker, E. and Tilton-Weaver, L. (2003). Who gets caught at maturity gap? A study of pseudomature, immature and mature adolescents. *International Journal of Behavioral Development.* 27(3) 253-266

90. Scalfari, E. (2013). The Pope: how the Church will change. *La Repubblica.* October

91. Bogan, J. (2009). America's biggest megachurches. *Forbes.* June 26

92. Camping, Harold. Familyradio.org

93. Banks, A. (2013). Harold Camping may be facing doomsday, but not the one he predicted. *Religion News Service* May 14

94. Svorak, P. (2009). D.C. Homeless people use cellphones, blogs, and e-mail to stay on top of things. *The Washington Post.* March 23

95. Ebert, R. (2012). We've seen this movie Before. *The New York Times,* July 20

96. Konrath, S.H., O'Brien, E. and Hsing, C. (2011). Changes in dispositional empathy in American college students over time: A meta-analysis. *Personality and Social Psychology Review* 15:180

97. Tyler, I. (2007). From the Me Decade to the Me Millennium: The cultural history of narcissism. *International Journal of Cultural Studies.* 10:343

35186525R00131

Made in the USA
Lexington, KY
01 September 2014